MW01171685

Paint.

Also by Erik De La Cruz:

Hert.

Paint.

By

Erik De La Cruz

Copyright © 2021 by Erik De La Cruz. All Rights Reserved.

Printed in the United States of America. No part of this book may be used or reproduced in any manner whatsoever without written permission except in the case of reprints in the context of reviews.

ISBN: 978-1-7334365-8-8

www.erikdelacruz.com

Concept: Erik De La Cruz
Editor: Omar Apodaca
Front and Back Cover Design: Javier De La Cruz
Interior Book Design and Layout: Erik De La Cruz

10 9 8 7 6 5 4 3 2 1

Contents

Chapter One

Reminders of Broken Love

Chapter Two

Nostalgia Lane

Chapter Three

Heart's Renaissance

Dedicated

To the *inner child* that has been forgotten — living amongst the gray.

I hope my words give you the colors to paint again.

"Stop trying to paint all women with the same brush!"

I'm just turning pain into colors.

Paint me as a villain, if you must.

Chapter One

Reminders of Broken Love

Most days I am a museum of things.

I want to forget,
The gallery of memories is haunting,
When you're the muse,
Within the museum of my mind,
Your beauty belongs within frames,
But your beauty caused me all these pains,
I can't handle the rains,
Despite knowing that with it comes growth,
The art that comes from you is priceless,
Ever since you left,
I've been a mess,
I want to forget... you,
But the things we did together,
Are worthy of being displayed...
In a museum.

What happened to us?

You were scared to let me in,
You never let me in,
Inside your heart,
Inside your hurt,
Inside your soul,
You carry so much within,
You never release it to anyone,
Not even the man you supposedly love...

Drunken nights, drunken fights,
You spill droplets of your upsets,
But it's never a big enough flow because of your dammed pain.

Excruciating yells and threats to leave,
Sunrises cause you to feel regrets,
Sun sets then it resets,
The scars continue to bleed,
But you hide the blood with tight clothes,
These bandages over our problems,
These emotions are under wraps,
These emotions released under sheets,
Then the cycle repeats.

True Love

She says she loves you,
She tells you each time you depart,
Of your life, she's become a huge part,
To have a woman truly love you,
It's not what she says,
It's not her words...
She must be capable of feeling great pain for you,
The more she's vulnerable,
The depth of her love becomes greater,
The feeling of love from you she wants forever,
That's not to say the intention to hurt her is there,
But you have the power to,
You can if you so wanted to,
That power to be held with honor,
You're careful because you love her,
At the mercy of your power,
She would have it no other way,
Because she genuinely loves you,
She'd rather be in agony at the thought of losing you...
Than actually losing you — so profound her love,
Love rooted in her actions,
She displays her love with her body,
She displays her love with acts of service,
It's not about what she says,
For fear is a stronger force than comfort,
For respect is to be had on her behalf,
Never settle for a love half of what it should be,
For without her admiration,
The love simply has an expiration.

The attachment to this fairy tale never ends well,
You begin to live a life of servitude towards love,
A devotion to an illusion where the sacrifice is you.

Love becomes your religion which wastes away your life's mission.

The memories get loud,
The memories knock on your door,
The memories leave tears on the floor.

Two drinks in,
You're thinking of us two,
Hoping to recreate what we used to,
Wondering if she feels me — like you used to,
Dying that I'm used to being without you.

Three drinks in,
Flashbacks of our three years,
Chasing away dark fears of losing me for good.

Four drinks in,
You're praying that you're still the love I'm looking for.

...

...

Calls and texts obsessively,
Begging for my kisses,
Begging for my forgiveness,
Fantasizing about the makeup sex,
But there's nothing to make up,
What's done is done,
You had your fun, you had your run,
Running out of time, your beauty is fading,
You're ugly when you're desperate.

Your ego becomes deflated once you get out there,
Never understood how well you had it,
Never understood your horrid habits,
Never could rid yourself of your desires,
Your looks are about to expire.

Gone is our fire and what we had,
You thought you could go bad,
Then expect for me to take you in with open arms,
Now that I have many women, I have choice,
Feelings and regrets you want to voice,
Alcohol always aided all of your misery,
But it never was about me or because of me,
Your shot glass, empty,
Your heart, empty,
Your father role, empty,
Your relationship with your mother, hollow,
You were someone I was bound to outgrow,
Your actions did the work for me,
Your actions awoke me,
No actions you do now could retain me.

Five drinks in,
Buzzing to the route of blacked,
There's no going back.

Devil's in the Details

I know your every quirk,
I know how much you love my laugh and smirk,
I know every inch of your skin,
I know what spots tickle, what spots turn you on,
I know your favorites,
Movies, shows, celebrities,
Even your various personalities,
I've learned every detail about you...

The change is sudden,
The change is hidden,
Your routines are thrown off,
You're rarely happy around me,
You're no longer the girl I fell in love with,
You're unrecognizable in every way,
You're finished with conversations before they even begin,
I surprise you with gifts, love, and... nothing,
You're avoidant, brief, sketchy,
Late work nights, last-minute plans,
You begin to put me last,
I did everything to make sure we last,
You treat me like I'm someone from your past in the now,
You're not the girl I fell in love with...

...

...

Who are you?
What did you do to the girl I love?
Where is what she was and everything I loved?
I wake up next to you but it's like you're gone,
A cold part of the bed, a blanket to myself,
Your body was here but your mind was elsewhere.
Feelings you used to feel with me, you get elsewhere,
Where else is your mind since it's not here with me?

Soon I realize,
There's someone else,
No wonder, you'd wander,
That must be the answer,
Of course, you deflect,
You lost respect, I lose respect for you,
You didn't communicate which led to my own self-hate,
I thought there was something wrong with me,
All when the reality is you found another,
The covers soon were taken away,
Bed empty, head empty, heart empty,
Leaving you with nothing to say,
I knew everything about you,
But I guess you changed,
And found a way to still surprise me,
Even at the cost of me.

Drowning Shadows

She gets lost,
Drugged out and high,
All for two seconds of euphoria,
Where it all goes silent,
Where her mind is at peace,
That's when it all felt right...

Then, that exhilaration is no longer there,
The fall is ungraceful,
The whirlwind is hurtful,
She chases that high constantly,
She spirals down constantly,
As she falls to the floor,
So does her tears,
When floating — away goes her fears,
The darkness wraps around her soul,
For the hug gives a false sense of hope,
That it has finally been contained,
Not realizing what she lost at such a young age,
Before the stress,
All she sought was her happiness.

Rue The Day

You're high,
I'm not sure who put you on this pedestal,
You ask me to come over only to start fights,
You figured you were right,
But your mind wasn't here,
It was elsewhere,
I don't even know where you were tonight,
Out of your mind,
You say the drugs help you unwind,
But all you do is wind up causing destruction,
You can't function, you blame me for everything.

Drugs gave you a way to get out of your head,
Drugs gave you a rush like I used to,
You started to do drugs, it took you away,
It helped you... or so you said,
Only to become addicted,
Drugs in the replacement of love,
You loved to do drugs,
You love the drugs more than anything,
Drugs took you away...
Took you away from me,
Took all of who you used to be,
A fiend for your next rush,
You were unrecognizable,
A new group of friends,
I knew you were lost for good,
In your own world, a lost girl,
I left you, I let you roam on your own,
There was no saving you,
You were always over dosing,
The high was never enough,
It's like you sought to overdose,
Because death was the ultimate high,
And each time you came close.

Only God can judge her,
Only God can punish her,
God only knows the sins she's committed,
God only knows the lies she's told men,
Lies she told to men to whom she was committed,
She never believed in God,
She loved the fallback of using God's name,
She loved to fall back on beds that weren't hers,
She loved to scream, "Oh my God!"
She never believed in God,
She evaded accountability,
She had an ability to account for dollars men spent on her,
She was an offering basket, passed through lines,
Her body filled with gold,
Poor men placing money in her basket,
She was wealthy, bread rose like a miracle,
Wine sipping the blood of these disciples,
She never received God's discipline,
A world of freedom, no repercussion,
God had faith in her,
But she never had faith in herself,
When there's no one to punish,
She punishes herself,
A life of sin, temporary wins,
Just to live in sorrow,
Because she only focused on the now,
Never in the tomorrow,
God knocks on her door.

Only when she's on the floor,
Wine drunk and alone,
Ready to be born again,
After being dead inside,
Expects a resurrection after falsified perfection,
Poor men assembled hoping to provide her salvation,
She became a religion for the broken.

This deceiving Eve,
With a wicked forked tongue,
Any lie — she makes you believe,
Smiles while you suffer,
The venom from her mouth as you kiss her,
Used her lips as weapons to bring you closer,
Her deception turned you into a lover.

The age of *uninnocence* is birthed.

A world where life is best lived through vices and the senses.

Malibu Models

She wants the endless summer,
She thirsts for the wetness of the ocean,
She wants to live in la la land,
Where it's all fun and ease,
Where all men give her attention and want to please,
Where all girls are envious of her preciousness,
She wants the endless summer,
Where she can roam half-naked and carefree,
Where the sand warms the coldness of her heart,
Where the sun tanned her skin,
Despite her already being dark within...

Unclouded her skies,
She rains with her pink skies,
For the forever youth entices her every vein,
Her blood boils at the thought that the summer ends,
For the fall causes her happiness to fall,
To her — clothed is no way to live at all,
The jackets restrain her freedom,
Straight to the jackets, her skin is frail,
The craziness rises as the summer's sunset falls,
She wants the endless summer,
Spends her life trying to hold time still,
Desperately, to keep something from ending,
She wanted to capture summer in fear of closure,
She feared the winds of her future,
That window of fun is narrow,
As time ticks, fun becomes less and less...
That does come to an end.

Pretty Privilege

All she ever knew was more than fine,
All she ever knew was she was fine,
All she ever knew was fine dining,
All was given to her,
All she ever lifted was herself out of bed,
All was catered and gifted,
All she ever did was turn heads,
All she ever did was get attention,
All I ever was to her was a blip,
All I could provide was me,
All she had was all she wanted,
All I could give was love,
All her beauty made me fall,
All she wanted her daddy provided,
All I could do is walk away,
All I did was stay — aware that I meant nothing,
All I could provide her was nothing,
All I could give her was my all,
All seemed fine,
All she did was break more hearts than mine.

All I ever wanted was the(se) blonde(s).

She's a part-time model and a part-time lover,
She only ever gives part of herself,
Never her full heart,
Despite being full of herself,
She blames all as she's tamed by nothing at all,
Reckless, ruthless, and shameless in her desires,
The round and round of the carousel,
Leaves temporary dizziness,
Where she assumes love she'd never miss,
Until time reflects the truth.

In her mind...
She's never in the wrong so she never changes.

What A Fool

You loved to be on your knees,
You loved to swallow...
My interests, qualities, and music taste,
Ingested them and off you went,
To another,
You acted as if they were always a part of you,
But the other is clueless to your finesse,
He finds you down to earth and cool,
Oh, what a fool,
The most down that you were to earth,
Was simply to be on your knees.

You acted brand new as you absorbed more,
Unrecognizable but still present was your devil,
You lured those who didn't see you for who you were,
Interests matched, got him thinking it's a perfect match,
But they were never you,
The real you was as blank as an unpainted canvas,
Oh, what a fool,
He'd be to think you were worth anything,
You didn't know anything, you didn't do anything,
Any things you knew didn't come...
From you,
Men came for you.

You loved it, made you more powerful,
The emptiness — you were seeking to make full,
The theft you pulled off to increase your palette,
Colors from the estranged donors,
You wanted to be more than just beautiful,
By any means necessary,
You wanted to add layers to your being,
You got tired of being nothing but a pretty face,
That's why your reflection you could never face.

Men came for your body,
You hoping they'd stay for something more,
But you became nothing more than a painting to glance at,
Briefly, before men walked away,
To see something else in the gallery.

Attention,
Blurred vision,
Crossed boundaries,
Dragging baggage,
Empty inside,
Future unseen,
Getting lost,
Hurt.

I'm falling just for the night,
Your guards fall just for the night,
Your panties fall lustfully for the night,
You fall into momentary love,
But when the sun rises so do, we,
And all that is left is nothing but a memory,
Categorized as a fun plummet,
Nothing comes from it,
We emotionally wane to stay sane,
We abstain from feeling to remain the same,
Neither of us leaves the same,
The constant numbness hidden under smiles,
We gravitated then dissipated,
Patterns of the brokenhearted.

//

Night after night for you they blended,
Faded you blushed, flirted then ghosted,
Your cycles were predictable,
To fall and become grounded was nothing but a fable,
How could she when all her friends do is enable horrible actions,
So they can be free from being labeled as judgmental,
All she knew was to run away from labels,
All she knew was to run away from titles,
Drinks made you feel free,
Tied to the chains of escape...

Conceal the real,
Concealer for the dark circles your life has become,
Pours of liquors cover pores from your face,
Smearless makeup to make up for the tears,
Avoiding herself in all these lost years,
Seeking to make up for her lost years,
Where only thoughts of innocence filled her,
For the damage was too far gone,
The blemishes cause loss of beauty,
The foundation of innocence is gone,
No use in trying to age in reverse,
The lack of soul is nothing you can make up.

All Girls Are The Same

The desire for real love is deep,
Deep within as it's hard to reveal to others,
There's a fear of being hurt,
Her look of innocence makes me want to give her my heart,
Giving her the power to destroy my innocence,
Giving her the power to break my heart,
She knew what she was doing,
I was just trying to be loving,
Giving her everything I could,
I imagined she was everything,
The kind of girl I dreamed of in my childhood,
The type of girl you'd see in romantic comedies,
That you'd imagine personified love,
Only to destroy every facet of it in your face.

...

...

Her need for attention was unattainable,
I was never enough when her phone brought all that and more,
The dopamine from the screen was obscene,
The attention she got was more than I could ever give her,
Hundreds liked her, if not thousands,
That were willing to give her diamonds,
No need to even be discreet,
I could never compete,
Her ego inflated,
We no longer related.

Caught up with the desire to never expire,
She felt that a day without sharing a picture,
Would cause her audience to forget she exists,
There's so much competition in social realms that it often overwhelms,
How could one man make her feel anything,
None of what I liked about her mattered,
None of the stories I shared with her mattered,
I wanted her heart,
She wanted the hearts of others,
Only for the emotion, she played each one,
She saw us as slaves that would feed her to her liking,
She was always exploring for the next trend or boyfriend,
New styles constantly, you're thrown away after a while,
I tried to influence her,
Despite the direct messages she never listened,
She only cared for more exposure,
She knew the angles to make her body angelic,
She knew her future lover was only ever a click away,
She got men to gaze — digital runway,
Girls these days attached to the digital window displays,
You'd think these girls were mazes that are unsolvable,
But truth is, they're leeching for attention,
Seeking fame more than love,
These girls are all of the above.

The Hills Have Lies

Small town girl with dreams,
Chases after the thrill,
Falls in love with the idea of the Hollywood Hills,
Fast lifestyle that she happily exchanges for her innocence,
Where she counts calories and loses count of drinks taken,
She runs towards an endless summer of sunsets and lives on Sunset.

Enticed by the glamor of Beverly Hills,
Her tastes of clothes and food elevate,
Tight dresses with friends that are actresses,
The chaos that ensues brings blues but she continues to pursue,
She wants fame, money, and attention,
She wants the cars, clothes, and craziness,
She wants the spa and pool days which rewards her laziness,
She wants to relax because being beautiful is exhausting,
Where she wishes flings turned into wedding rings,
Extravagant weddings and mansions,
To play house with the man of her dreams,
But accept none of the responsibility of being a wife,
Her life is made and has maids taking care of the cleaning,
Nannies raising her kids because she can't handle the stress,
More important are trips to the country club where she has to impress,
She obsesses over being perceived as a good mom instead of being one.

She immersed herself in the hills where she never pays bills,
This time it's those of Malibu, where wealth is too good to be true,
She used to have no curfews,
Now she's blessed with house crews.

...

...

Pretty ocean views,
Petty emotional issues,
Soon the unhappiness continues,
Where she seeks rendezvous to diffuse,
Never satisfied, she plays around with the idea of a new man to choose,
She's tired of the waves, they've come to a standstill.

She wants to go where the celebrities live in the Hidden Hills,
Lavish lifestyles of the rich and famous,
Lavish lifestyles of the broken and dangerous.

She wants it all,
Divorce is the natural course which her friends endorse,
She wants to feel young and hot once more with no remorse,
Hefty sums of money and property make her happy,
She knows the courts will give her amnesty for being lonely,
A world that aids her ability to have it all,
A new life without the need of a man,
Despite a man being the one to fund it,
She can now—with men—only focus on the fun of it,
No need to look for someone to rescue her,
She goes back to living through the blur,
Wine nights, tequila shots, and hard seltzer,
Back to nepotism and a life solely for pleasure.

A small town girl who was once a treasure...
Because of her environment she became a disaster.

Inside, she dreams of going back home.

She loves to fall for the bad ones,
She hates to fall for the bad ones,
She's tied to her wiring,
The strings pull her towards the bad ones,
She's a puppet to her wiring,
Her vices are the master she's tied to…
She's infatuated by the lust,
Gives herself fully to someone she doesn't fully trust,
But she could care less,
She's careless with her heart when it comes to the bad ones.

The heartless bad ones,
She wants to give her heart to,
The good ones she pays no mind,
They are not even ever on her mind,
The bad ones are good enough for her,
They are the ones that are distant enough,
That she must chase, she loves the bad cycles,
She loves the good rush from the bad ones,
She loves the butterflies from the lies,
She pretends they're half-truths,
Justifying her own naivety.

...

...

The sensations are too good for the temptations to leave,
The tingles defeat the idea of being single,
Attracted and attached to the distress,
As he doesn't even bother to impress you,
He still swoons you with his lack of care,
He's different than the men that are desperate for you,
The roles reversed towards him,
Something you're not used to,
You love to hate the chase,
You hate the space he gives you,
But his non-neediness is what drives your obsession,
From your first impression of him, it left you with sexual tension,
Something you had no explanation for,
Something you've never felt before,
But once you got a taste of the bad ones you wanted more,
Your addiction became apparent — you had no shame,
You didn't even care if he forgot your name,
To capture his heart and change his bad ways was your aim,
Within you that challenge sparked your flame,
You knew you were trapped by his charm and game,
You didn't care because this feeling was rare,
You acted like one of the good ones to grab his attention,
But you wanted to be a bad one just for him,
That was your mission.

Free Herself

You were someone I never should've known...
Who just loved to destroy as you go,
Who never felt you deserved what you had,
You loved to play good on the exterior,
But you were bad and it rotted your interior,
You had ulterior motives,
You used me in all ways you could think of,
I realized I was never in love and neither were you,
You pretended till the second it ended and then your facade fell,
It instantly turned to stone as no emotion was expressed at all,
You acted like I was someone you'd never known,
You never allowed yourself to feel anything,
You never stopped running from distress,
The stress of having to impress everyone.

You could never show or let anyone know that your life wasn't perfect,
That you had perfect looks, body, and life,
Thoughts of being a wife brought nausea,
Reflections of parents breaking up and the drama,
She carried the misfortunes of her parent's divorce,
Parents argued on behalf of her so she carried fault and remorse,
As a little girl, she'd hear the yelling leaving their voices hoarse,
The next day, eyes swollen, she'd hear, "Good morning!"

She sought solace from boys,
Immediately understood she wasn't going to follow their course,
The deep attention she yearned for — she got from intercourse,
Couldn't face feelings, mom and dad left her off course,
Spent her entire life detaching so she wouldn't repeat their patterns,
Something she probably never unlearns...

That's when I knew the torment in her heart's source,
We were never meant to complement as it wasn't even time well spent,
Feelings of any type, she'd always prevent,
At least then, she'd free herself from disappointment.

Venom of the System

You got me feeling emotionless,
Dead — the emotions you bring me,
The sex is what it is,
No feeling at all,
I'm moving on before even moving anything,
There's no moving of any sensation,
Quick lust, temporary trust,
Quick thrust, quick bust,
Neither of us feeling anything,
You're filling holes while filling holes,
You're filling holes while filling voids,
You're filling voids while feeling boys,
I was nothing but a spark of sensation,
I'm filling holes while filling voids,
You were nothing to me but a release to relax,
Playing the same game with no shame,
A game for sinners with no winners,
You move cold, emotionless before and post,
You move sexy, emotions expressed during sex,
Numb becomes the outcome.

Listening to the system's venom,
Accustomed to the momentum,
Building a romanticism to the escapism,
Ironically avoiding self,
When you're fueled by solipsism,
It's in your nature, your algorithm,
Just a machine for your benefit,
Never been the type of girl to submit nor commit,
Less emotion leaves you ready at any moment to split,
No remorse, no guilt,
Foundation built to fall,
Neither of us meant anything to each other at all.

Falling for the Chaos

In the shadows, we play with fire,
Round after round, we never tire,
We love the chaos that ensues from our trust issues,
Both of us at a distance while we hold each other's bodies,
Refraining from feelings, both using each other for entertainment,
The treasure of us is simply the pleasure,
Late-night messages turn into late-night ménage à trois,
Me, you, and the covers,
More and more comfortable, we understand each other's bodies,
The orgasmic ecstasy leaves us in awe,
But as quick as it comes, we leave,
We can't leave the lingering potential to simmer,
Feelings that boil would spoil the heat of the summer,
Evade emotions because they come with trouble,
Both unsure of what would come of us if the bubble bursts,
We both become aware of the subtleties,
The holding of hands becomes a second longer than it should,
The kisses goodbye become more intimate which we both hate,
We begin to see our barriers crumble,
We begin to see ourselves for each other stumble,
I think we're both falling...

You begin to worry who I'm with late at night,
I begin to worry about the trivial which starts a fight,
Jealousy begins to creep, love from our skin begins to seep,
But we both know this can't be because we made rules,
Promise to never fall — promised to never be each other's all,
Only to give each other an escape and excitement,
Riskier and riskier texts begin to be sent,
Come overs become sleepovers,
Deep lovers into an official title?
We broke every rule we had,
Never a couple, we're supposed to stay casual,
Both fearful, afraid of the emotional hassle,
Both scared of the fun becoming flammable,
Aware of the magical and pitiful that comes with relationships,
Why be fearful when there's so much potential,
Let's just relax and let go in our heads,
Let's just fall — the same way we laid on a bed,
Screw whatever... we said.

Numb(er)

I fell in love,
She told me that was a personal problem,
Because it was never love,
She was playing the game,
She loved to be numb,
Alcohol, drugs, and entertainment,
She continued to carry on with her life,
I attempted to carry on our relationship,
She said it never existed, she just liked the sex,
But she is now looking for whatever is next.

I vilified her as heartless,
She told me after being used so many times...
She started using her heart less.

She flirted with the idea of commitment,
Kept you chasing for something that was never meant for us,
She could pick and choose to her liking,
A player but somehow, she managed a roster,
Knew the game, all the strategies, and was always three moves ahead,
Her face would leave you breathless,
Her brain would leave you speechless,
Her smile would leave you powerless,
Her body would make you nervous,
I fell in love and there was never an "us,"
She mocked my misery after she said she doesn't feel the same,
She said I was the one to blame,
My fault for finding no fault in her,
For thinking that there was a future,
The only thing on her mind was her future,
Nothing could get in her path,
She enjoyed pleasure and money,
It was never love nor starting a family,
She chose herself before anything else,
Never realizing careers wither,
Now, no one wants to be with her,
Never realizing that all of that was temporary,
Especially her beauty that soon was overrun by her ugly personality,
What once gave her freedom to reign hell,
Became what made her alone and within a tormented jail.

Unfortunate Consequence

Look what I did...
Look what I created,
I ruined your heart,
I left you for dead,
Now you stay up crying all night in bed,
Now out of spite, you lay strangers in your bed,
Now I don't recognize who you've become,
You were pure and loveable,
Now you're insecure and just fuckable,
Your innocence vanished once you were damaged,
Am I to blame?
For taking advantage of genuine love,
For entertaining other women,
After you found out, you were never the same,
Am I to blame?

You got cold and secretly boiled inside,
Then the weather warmed up as the summer came,
You got hot and went out with your girls,
Tight dresses to mess with my head,
Unrecognizable you became,
What a shame that you became hollow,
I took your heart and shattered it,
So, you spent drunken nights trying to bandage the pain,
Around town, you had sudden fame,
The girl who was no longer tamed nor chained,
Free from the burden of a relationship,
You just enjoyed the pleasure and the fun,
The worst part is that you have just begun,
The attention without expectations,
The temptations without distractions,
A free girl with a vengeance,
Who in a bad world never stood a chance.

...

...

You loved the chaos,
I ruined you,
I created chaos,
My greatest loss,
I try not to care but I see you...
So sad pretending that you're happy,
The girl you once were is gone forever,
I'm not sure if I'll ever have better,
A girl with such a promising future,
Became a walking disaster with such carelessness...
She didn't care for her future,
Only cared for the moment,
Look what I did...

Did I birth this dilemma?
Or was it always someone you were meant to become?
Something you had inside that you hid from me?
Was I the inception?
Or was the whole thing a deception?
Was it always who you were?
Or was it because I destroyed your hope and what made you pure?
I will never be sure because you're no longer mine,
I loved you but that wasn't enough,
I broke your trust,
Ultimately, breaking you,
You claimed you were fine,
But I knew you rampaged while enraged at me,
You've lost who you used to be,
Nothing would fix what I did, not even a sorry,
You were forced to live unhappy because of your spite towards me,
Amid all your crazy acts,
All I can do now is... look at what I did.

Out of Her System / After the Fun

She enjoyed the fun that came with the party years,
She wasted time and had many wasted times,
She loved the exhilaration of what kind of guy she would meet,
She never imagined you to be the guy she'd meet,
Her years declining, credit cards declining,
She ran her course, ready for the pit stop,
The party years,
The alcohol, drugs, and sex she loved,
The breaking of her heart for years,
The boys that used her, for her worth, that she loved,
The shedding of so many tears,
She bounces back, falls on your lap,
She's got it all out of her system,
She's ready for the reset and to start anew with you,
You've heard some of the stories, it was a part of her life,
She doesn't know "her" anymore,
She disassociates with that image of herself,
As far as she could tell, it never happened,
No need to worry she tells you,
Out of her system.

You just bought into her epiphany,
Phased by her beauty,
Her life once consisted of more than just pounding—
Shot glasses on the counter,
Rendezvous in bathroom stalls,
Where for her time would stall,
And she'd inside her want it all,
While you get no affection at all,
Do the chores, take the kids, run the errands,
All of a sudden, you're "sexy" and she rewards you,
A trained animal she keeps you as,
A man cave you create to make you feel manly,
Only to realize it's how she keeps you as a pet,
The house you pay for and she becomes the master.

...

...

She allows you to watch games,
She allows you to drink a few beers,
You ask for permission to hang out with your friends,
While you're out she's blowing you up to come back home,
You're stuck, invested, and for the damage she has you paying interest,
The debt she accrued during her party years,
The early 20's of her rampaging for attention,
An era that destroyed her purity,
The habits morphed over time to girl's nights and wine,
For all you know, overtime at work is where she discharges her desires,
A work husband, a work boyfriend reaping the benefits,
While you're raped by the bills you pay for — with no benefits,
She's got friends with benefits while you're stuck with the expenses,
Stuck, unfucked, and cucked.

Your life is a disaster, you thought you could save a party girl,
But the girl who loves to party never misses a party,
Girls like her just want to have fun,
She got someone to give her kids,
And fund her lifestyle,
Girls like her just want to have fun(ds),
You're left helpless in distress,
You allowed yourself to get played,
This is enough to get suicidal,
She wanted the fun, marriage, then hide the fun,
She wanted it all,
All was temporary to her, but what truly drove her was the party,
She was never meant to be taken into your home,
A stray that loves to play,
More than just play with your heart and emotions,
All that wasted time...
Thinking you found someone worth raising a family with,
She could never respect a man that chose to settle with her,
Because she always respected the men that left her.

Devil Wears Designer

It was never enough,
Love, care, money, food,
It was never enough,
She smiled like it was enough,
The last of my money went for her to eat,
I would starve as my insides carved themselves,
Hour-long bus rides for minutes with her — just to repeat,
Genuine in my love, in my care,
I attached my happiness to hers,
Those moments were everything,
The minor details you spoke I would save in my back pocket,
The lengths I would go to show I remembered,
Spending each dollar I had in my back pocket,
You were there for me when I was poor,
Money came in abundance, I taught you designer dances,
I worked... for you, I put you first,
It was never for me as your happiness was first,
It was never enough,
I was young, I saw kids with you,
You saw us as just kids,
Needing to grow without me,
She didn't want to repeat the steps of her mother,
She didn't want to repeat the steps... so she stepped on me,
She didn't want to repeat the steps of her mother,
I loved how our hands fit perfectly together,
I gave her a year for each finger on my hand,
I felt the pain of each finger of yours slipping away,
Her focus shifted to herself, she needed time,
Her love shifted to herself, she selfishly needed time,
My love was never enough,
My care for her meant nothing... like it never happened,
My love ceased to exist in her devilish eyes,
Her love turned into a charity, stuck for the sake of pity,
She stopped loving me?
She never loved me?

...

...

She whispered there were hard times — that were pretty lies,
Hard times came from carrying me around,
Like an out of season accessory,
She got bored of me, just to leave me,
She saw no issue in leaving me to die, alone,
Malnourished, never cherished,
I ran to alcohol where I would rather die,
Our entire span was just a lie.

She pushed away the one that loved her most,
She sought to escape in what else is out there,
My drive almost led me to my death,
Failed to realize the free way could bring more than death,
Failed to realize this never would have lasted,
Thousands spent on makeup couldn't make up the holes in your heart,
She couldn't commit, made herself lost looking for love she had,
But it was never enough,
I gave her everything, anything she wanted,
To be just like any thing that was in her closet,
Everything meant nothing,
Having nothing I realized I gave her what I never had,
Love, care, money, food,
Suddenly, I had that for myself in abundance,
My mom saw her son dance,
After the darkness of the sunset,
Darkness showed me the pain of almost settling,
Darkness made the man,
Darkness made me heartless,
Now, I keep that in my back pocket,
Where no girl knows, a secret,
I am better, happier, healthier,
It kills her inside, reach out she's tried,
But I am no longer tied,
For what I did for her was never enough,
What I did for me post-her was more than enough,
It took losing you to realize what I had inside,
Because what I did for myself is more than what you would do by my side.

Letter Home

What a mess of emotions as I leave a tearful letter,
To the girl that wanted, pursued, loved, and got me…
But you never actually got me while I got "her."

I gave too much to the first one,
Without the first — there's no second,
There's no you.

You fell in love with my potential,
You waited for personal gain,
Heartbreak hurts but potential hurts even more,
I poured so much love into you but it was never enough,
I, too, believed I could fully fall in love, but I never did,
Despite the beautiful bubble we lived in,
It was always just for the meantime.

You said your whole heart was mine…
You acted single the entire time you were with me,
You felt cheated when I left… but I was cheated on,
All this hurt came from your temporary highs,
I hope it was worth it now that you're alone,
I hated so many things about you but my love overlooked it all,
I was entangled and fell for the allure of false hopes,
I was the only person who knew you for you…
That saw the potential in you that you didn't see in yourself,
Now, you keep yourself busy to hide your sadness,
What kept you from crying and screaming all at once,
As you never loved any man like you loved me.

I loved you more than any man ever could,
But you never felt worthy, so you self-sabotaged,
The damage left — left me wanting to kill myself…

Here I am forgiving you…
While never wanting to see or hear from you again,
This letter, as these letters say goodbye for good,
Cheers to what could've been,
A toast of champagne without pain,
I'm glad I chose to runaway,
I've found happiness away from you.

The Worst of Me and You

Her motions,
Her actions,
Her emotions,
All out of spite.

Everything was done in the wrong mindset,
You did it with the thought that you were in the right,
The constant suffering, I endured,
The constant change I attempted to make in you,
The only constant was the constant misery you brought me,
The frustrations that boiled within me,
The yelling I did in hopes that you'd hear me,
No matter how near, your ear never picked up my words,
All out of spite,
Fighting was the only thing I could do to keep your attention,
You were seeking attention in all places but with me,
The constant war through texts,
At least then, I knew you weren't cheating, maybe,
The ease it brought me—that at that second—you were with me,
The constant battles in person,
Your eyes looked away, your body turned away,
Besides each other facing opposite directions in bed,
Even the tears weren't loud enough as they fell,
I fought hard because I saw the potential change in you,
You fought back because you didn't like the idea I had of you,
You acted out of spite,
I sought to help you better yourself,
You sought to destroy us, so you didn't have to change,
You hated that I saw you as something more than you,
I fought because I was afraid of change,
I fought to stay because I wasn't ready to find the undamaged and new,
You never wanted better, you just wanted new,
I couldn't force you to change when you wanted to remain unmoved,
I loved you and cared for you,
But even that changed when I found my value.

Dream Man / Bad Kind of Butterflies

She can't sleep, tossing and turning,
Thinking of him and her tossing and turning,
While you lay right beside her,
She hides all these parts of her from you,
She opens all parts of her for him,
Every waking moment spent thinking of the past moments,
She can't get any sleep,
It kills her softly that her love is elsewhere while he's elsewhere,
And you're right beside her but bring nothing but a bore,
She texts him secretly, thoughts of him make her high,
He could care less about her,
She wished he cared more so she loves the challenge,
She's already conquered you... who's there for her on a whim.

She wants to fight for him,
He sees her for what she is, you see her as something more,
Backwards — but she loves it,
In a panic, you start doing the little things you did in the beginning,
You're going backward in time trying to make up for lost time,
You sense that her mind isn't here with you,
You go above and beyond,
She can't think anything beyond him being above her,
You've lost a battle you can't even see,
She doesn't want you to see,
Her dream man is in her reality, she can't sleep,
You've become a present nightmare despite all your care,
She loves keeping him on the low,
Her emotions she kept cocooned,
The secret excites and makes her feel a bad kind of butterflies,
But she opens the cage, allows them to fly.

...

...

Weightless she feels, heartless she is,
Tosses your emotions aside,
Turning your life upside down instantly,
She risks the relationship with you, for one with him,
She awaits the right moment to reach out for the new branch,
Waiting on the impending avalanche of chaos,
Everything destroyed, everything's a loss,
No loyalty she ever had,
You can't sleep, tossing and turning,
Thinking of her and him together,
Tossing, turning, and crying.

You thought you found the right girl,
But she left you because she had someone else to find,
To her, you were nothing more than temporary,
And what was keeping her behind.

Outside Amusement

Falling out of love...
In darkness, you're letting him touch your skin,
Falling into love...
In darkness, I'm texting how much I love you,
Falling out...
You wanted out of my life,
... of love.
I had so much for you, but you were ready to give to another,
I gave you everything, years of me devoting,
All for your tears on his shoulder — leads to us eroding,
How did that shoulder to cry on...
Turn into something that turned you on?

You let him, you allowed it, you wanted it,
I wore my heart for you on my sleeve,
You wore less and let him slide your shirt off your arms,
Arms up, ready for the (emotional) rollercoaster,
Off the rails you had me,
I gave you everything and to you that was nothing,
Nothing worth staying for,
You loved his compassion and attention,
All he cared about was getting in,
Getting you out of my grasp,
He won and got you,
I didn't lose, you lost me,
I gained more than the loss of you,
I realized that you were no prize — that was just my jaded eyes,
Your actions allowed me to see the real you,
I fell out of the delusion... you had me in.

I ended up alone,
But after healing from the grief that I endured,
In which time was the cure,
I will be the one who wins,
Because when all is said and done,
You fell for the freedom's allure,
Where after the fun there is no savior,
You'll end up lonelier and insecure,
Because the love I had for you was pure,
And something you'll never recover.

She'd rather hurt from familiar pain,
Than live in a state of same with you.

Split Personality

She was sweet, playful, full of fun,
She was mesmerizing in her personality,
She radiates happiness, loves to be flirty,
She was mine so I never worried,
Things began to become shaky,
She started to act distant,
I ended things after years of attempts,
Her demeanor shifted entirely,
Struggled to find the meaning of her complete flip,
The relationship we had was valuable,
But quickly those years never mattered,
And my greatest fears brought tears...

She became vengeful,
Stone in her heart and in every bone,
Dark her soul became with no shame,
Tactfully slept with men,
That I thought were my true friends,
Out of spite, it wasn't right,
Thirsty fake friends followed suit,
Hoping to be the one to see her in her birthday suit,
Where she'd blow more than a candle,
The ugly thoughts I couldn't handle,
The appalling rumors I couldn't handle,
It broke me deeply,
Repulsively grim in her every action,
A gruesome grin she had with her every action,
Unlike her old self in every facet,
Her being became beyond awful,
Where I once saw beautiful...

...

...

It's haunting what you became,
Once released from commitment,
I couldn't prevent the resentment,
My induced pain from the indulges of your pleasure,
Shattered into pieces from your avenges,
All I could do for myself is reinvent,
I had to look inward and forget you,
Erase my so-called friends that entertained you,
All I had was myself, after all, is said and done,
I could no longer trust and I began to harden,
As time passed you were forgotten,
The addiction to your affection was no longer my destruction,
Due to my affirmation to become unbroken,
Who is there to blame?
Myself?
A girl who played a part?
Friends who were more desperate for pussy than they cared for loyalty?

All I had was me,
No longer could I trust easily, but I was happy with just me.

Beautiful Serenade

I endured enough emptiness every day with you,
I wept every night while you slept,
I wanted to end it,
You told me to shut up and you're not in the mood to handle it,
I pleaded to you to save me,
My mind strangled me where I had no breath left,
The waves crashing on the shore, I couldn't take it anymore,
Ending it all appealed to me more than life,
You begged and begged for me to open up,
I did on a final whim,
I bawled tears, expressed fears, regretted years,
You with a straight face, a dash of sentiment,
Enough to make it seem like you care,
I gave you my full emotion,
You told me generic things when I needed you to be genuine,
On your shoulder crying, as you wished to be elsewhere,
You couldn't take this, or take us,
You wouldn't listen, so you fake it,
My mental collapsed on every level,
"Just end it all," whispers the devil,
You were an accomplice with your actions,
You'd seen the man of your life wish for death,
You saw the weakness, the distress, and your love turned less.

...

...

Instead of checking on me, you began wrecking me,
Indirectly, as your intentions raised to the surface,
You began to look for a replacement,
The emotional brought you disgust and discontent,
"How could the man that's supposed to protect me be so pathetic?"
Your inner thoughts rang loud,
I should've known better,
You don't care, it's in your nature,
You say you do, but your actions speak otherwise,
You flirted with other men whenever you had a chance.

I wanted to kill myself and you used that as a reason to find yourself.

It took every ounce of me to not end it all,
Any bridge I passed by gave me a beautiful serenade to come fall,
I hardened, never pardoned, just learned,
I never forgave, I became smarter,
I never gave up, I never opened up again.

My rock cracked, my mental cracked,
Her waves need something hard to hit against,
The respect depleted, but she stuck around,
Soon I found myself and on my own built myself back up,
I played a part because I couldn't deal with a broken heart,
She wants to be the emotion,
A weak man doesn't bring a woman's devotion,
I recouped her love, but it taught me a lesson — to strengthen,
Then, I broke her heart once I found my mission.

Damaged Frame

She used to love me so effortlessly,
She would bring radiant energy,
Everywhere she would go, I'd love to go,
The conversations and moments we shared,
The passions under covers we shared,
Quickly, you became my favorite,
You loved that at first,
You love the attention and details I would remember,
Soon after, you became absent,
Just looking at me brought resentment,
It brought you pity that I was so weak,
You became my every goal and purpose,
No longer did I focus on me and my studies,
I just wanted to study every part of you,
I wanted to learn your entire history.

I wanted to solve all your issues,
I wanted to reconnect you with your father,
I strove to solve all those issues,
You tried but your father just broke your heart more,
He was never going to change,
He gave you all this false hope which broke you more,
I tried to bandage each wound with my lips,
I would wrap you with my arms in ways he never did,
I was so lost trying to fix broken things that shattered...
Before I was even in the picture.

...

...

Your dad lied to you,
Your dad used you as a weapon towards your mother,
You became his soldier taking verbal bullets for him,
By the time I met you, you had started to bleed to death,
I met the ghost of who you once were,
The innocence that was once there,
All of what you used to be had vanished,
I showed up trying to heal you,
Only for you to leave me punished,
How could you respect me...
When the only love you've ever experienced was cold,
I was a warmth that brought you discomfort,
You played along with me,
You let me attempt to play savior.

But you always knew that you were dragging me along,
Through the shattered glass of your family picture frame...

I was temporary while she ran circles,
I could never save her.

Whispers of Forever

She said, "I'm all yours…"
She wanted to give herself to me,
She said, "It's all yours…"
Her mind, body, and soul,
She'd never felt this type of way before,
It scared her but she loved the danger,
She wanted me in her life in all ways,
I asked her if I could come inside,
She opened all her doors for me,
I felt right at home,
She was devoted to building with me,
She wanted nothing more than to see me happy,
I heard her whispers of wanting forever,
I'm devoted to creating a legacy of forever,
She doesn't care, she just wants to be close,
She doesn't want to be left behind,
She wants to start a family,
Her need for my seed and last name,
That's her life's calling,
My deep desire to start a dynasty,
The enticement of such commitment,
But the constant dissonance of her being worth it or not,
The fear of giving her exactly what she wants.

…

...

She'll take what she needs,
And leave me to pay for a lifetime of the deeds,
Is she trustworthy?
Is she worthy of being trusted with my last name?

Is she to be trusted with the family secrets?
Could she handle the pressure?
Would she be a disaster that calls for our erasure?
The most important aspect is if she's pure,
Where her innocence is like a cure.

Is she free from the indoctrination of our nation?
Can she sacrifice the temptation for our union?
The temptation to become broken,
Where every moment we'd strengthen rather than poison,
Where we'd raise a wonderful daughter and a son,
A graceful divine daughter and a strong poised son,
The number of kids would be endless as we're limitless,
I fear her finesse, because I obsess with the success,
A second of looking away from my goal could be detrimental,
I just want to be secure and cared for with my mental,
An escape rather than someone overflowing with the sentimental,
She wants to give me her all,
Maybe I should give her my all,
She's great to me, wants me, and makes me happy,
I should remove the thought of a potential downfall,
But stay aware of the chance — no matter how small,
Take a risk and see if she's one for the long haul.

When Was It Over?

Was it when I said I couldn't hang out with you?
When I said no to hanging out with your friends?
Was it when I put my dreams before you?
When I went out with my friends instead of comforting you?
Was it when I cried in front of you?
When I told you I wanted to commit suicide — begging you to save me?
Was it when your insecurities bled into all my friendships with girls?
When I told you that I loved you?
Was it all those nights we fought?
When I ran from the seriousness of this relationship?
Was it when you did the same?

When was it over?
When you found another lover?
When did you know that it was time to leave?
When did the final piece inside your heart break?
That you knew you had to leave...
I can't bear the unknown,
I can't handle the lack of closure,
You were cold, held your composure,
You checked out early before the problems arose,
Could you not handle the genuine love I had for you?
You had it all in front of you,
Chose to chase after something unknown,
Having it all figured out so early scared you,
While the rest of your friends were lost,
You missed being lost with them,
You had found what was good for you,
But it wasn't enough to fill your needs,
You said I wasn't paying you enough attention,
When I gave you every moment I had,
When I told you I missed being by your side,
You couldn't handle the suffocation,
So you needed space to breathe,
Leaving me in a vacuum,
When was the moment that you knew you were through with me?

...

...

I can't seem to pinpoint because we were good together,
But you wanted something nonexistent and claimed was better,
You left me alone while you chased new experiences,
This level of pain was a new experience for me...
You made it look so easy,
You had it planned out beforehand,
You left before I could ask your father for your hand,
I saw forever with you and that scared you,
We were so young but I wanted no one else,
You wanted to try everything else before you got old.

The misery of this story told,
The mystery of our story untold,
So, when was it over?
When you thought you could do better?
When you fell out of love and fell silent in communication?
When you wanted attention elsewhere besides me?
Was it when my true love became boring to you?
The fact that you never had to chase my love anymore?
You knew you'd walk out on me eventually,
Why didn't you warn me?
I wish you did; I wish you had the decency,
Instead of leaving me in agony,
Leaving me with this overwhelming guilt as if I did something wrong,
When in reality, you became bored,
You claimed I made you feel alone in our relationship,
But you sought any excuse to leave,
You couldn't handle pure love,
It's not what you've ever experienced,
So, you chose to run away.

So, when was it over?
I guess, it doesn't matter,
Since in your mind,
We never started.

Routine Flashbacks

I miss when you would say my name,
I love when you would scream my name,
I didn't love when you would yell my name...
Out of fury over whatever pettiness you felt that day.

The moments we would cuddle on the couch,
The second your mom said good night...
That would spark our lust for each other,
Making out with no hesitation,
I miss how your face would look after my kisses,
I miss your smile after I made you laugh,
I would get under your skin,
But you'd love it,
It would lead to being under the sheets,
The pleasure we could never measure,
Young love,
There was nothing above,
We wanted nothing but each other,
I miss that sometimes,
Until we got sick of each other,
I tend to forget that part.

You wanted something else out of life,
As you were too young to be serious,
I wanted to give you everything in this life,
As I was too young to see the phase you were in,
Young love.

...

...

I was so naive at the thought we could last forever.

You only thought about your own future,
What was pure rotted,
I saw you as innocent but you wanted to experience,
At the time, none of it made sense,
But I realized that you fell out of love,
New feelings arose elsewhere,
Old feelings arise in the now for you,
I'm attached to that emotion,
I haven't felt that since so I reminisce,
Everything I did for you was out of love,
But you chose yourself above us,
Ever since us, I haven't been able to trust women the same,
You changed with me but ultimately stayed the same,
Oh, how lovely the irony,
Over you, over us,
I'd say you were my favorite but you were just my first,
I dream about what we could've been,
But you threw our love into a trash bin,
These cycles I go through remembering only the good,
When I shouldn't think about you at all,
We went our own paths,
I'm doing well after the hell you put me through,
Flashbacks of our love are what I'm sick of too,
Glad I'm over you.

Etched Memories

How long will you stay?
Even though you've already left...

How long do your memories stay?
How long will you be etched in my memory?
How long will I feel the ache in my heart?

You were the purest love I'd ever felt,
You made me the happiest I've ever felt,
I wanted to give you everything and more,
I couldn't wait to build a foundation for us,
We were young and in love,
The relationship got old to you,
You fell out of love,
Chose to leave me alone with no one to hold,
I didn't even catch that I was losing you,
I dropped everything as you were leaving,
Trying to do everything to win you back,
I wanted to keep us,
Our chemistry was the ultimate synchrony.

I was left broken...
You claimed that you broke slowly during our relationship,
Till you had no choice but to leave,
I gave you all my love and money — the last of what I had,
But you had to leave, you told me with no regret in your voice,
I watched you drive away as my heart imploded,
The most excruciating agony I've ever felt,
Piece by piece of my heart dropped to my stomach,
I felt sick, dropped to the floor — bawled.

...

...

The torment has stayed for years,
The pain since has never been solved,
How long will you have power over me?
How long until I forget you?
I wish I knew how long you'd linger in my mind,
Will it be when I find someone that makes me feel more than you?
Why can't I find someone that makes me feel more than you?
Will I be chasing emptiness until I die?
I've suffered for too long,
I need to bury our memories,
So, that you're dead to me...
You disappear from my thoughts,
You fade away forever from my memory.

Unfinished Modern Art

All I wanted,
All I wanted was her,
All I wanted was her to be happy with me.

All I wanted was greatness,
All she wanted was stillness...

I'd rather leave towards the unknown, what I don't know,
Than wait around for her to grow.

I had to let her go with a lot of pain in my heart.

An unfinished love...
I threw myself into work,
I threw the agony into creation,
Not so much the creation of anything but the recreation of myself,
The imagination and origination of ideas healed cuts,
Mental torment brought out what I was meant to do.

I started learning everything,
After learning that love isn't what it seems,
What got me through romantic pain was the romance...
of working towards my dreams.

These aloe vera sentences healed the scars.

Scared to open again.

Is the pain worth the potential gain?

Get Away

Her inclination to fall in love,
Clinging to me no matter what I do,
Her craze for me brings amazement,
She's heard rumors of my success,
With women and writing,
Writing about these women,
Now, these women write to me,
These women right their wrongs,
So, I can only see their righteousness,
Then, they could get me to write about their wrongs,
Just so they could brag to their girls that they mused a poem,
When she reads these lovely lines, she's so amused...
It's never just one anymore,
She's not special,
You always wanted to feel important,
But only ever for yourself,
For your benefit and attention,
You used and abused my time and attention,
Should've known the ulterior motives,
Her greed fueled her needs,
With her lust for fame, she brought no shame,
Acclaim through me was her aim,
Messages overlooked, I had to go away,
She wanted to stay, not just in my life and heart,
But forever in my art.

I'm in love with nothing but nostalgia.

Chapter Two

Nostalgia Lane

El Camino a Casa

This odyssey begins in the middle of things,
At my lowest point seeking to win,
A time beyond living memory.

On this odyssey, I seek prosperity.

These paths of my past,
Decades lost in the darkest of waters.

Wandering within waters,
No longer swimming but on a ship,
Hardships became easy and then revealed were the ships,
Convoy without hurt amongst the sea,
Conceal my identity to see who's real.

A homecoming by sea,
Land and see,
The homecoming by seeing land,
The constant crises causing cursed shipwrecks,
The perils and parts of me killed along the journey,
The greatness of surviving the journey as not many do.

These wrecks led to the blessing of friendships,
Encounters with beings close to the Gods,
Discovering I'm in a world beyond man,
Beyond the mortal universe,
Their influence overpowers will, if not careful.

I know thyself now,
Need not to return home rather I choose glory,
As I am destined to die as a poet.

My life is nothing but an epic poem,
Invoke inspiration—
"Muse, tell me in verse of the man of many wins."

My homeland once at me — laughed,
Now, my home rejoices that I saved myself,
For on this dreamland, I built a raft with my craft.

I laugh at those who didn't see me as the hero,
When lost, I feared the wrong decision at the crossroads.

Within the winds were the codes,
I fear nothing on this odyssey of dark roads.

The Mind's Fog

The strongest force which I lay victim to is nostalgia,
I allow it to take over my mind,
I succumb to the allure,
I imagine only of the pure,
Why I fall every time I'm never sure.

I dream of times where joy was present,
The world matured while praying that I didn't,
I didn't want the future to come so sudden,
The moments I cherished became fleeting,
Suddenly, I couldn't feel a thing,
I became numb as I bled the last of my sorrow,
What made me happy faded as seconds passed,
Nothing is worth living for when what was... is dead,
The contamination spread within my head,
I wish I could focus on the now instead,
I may never learn to...
As the next second leads to my deathbed.

Flashes Overlaid

Life goes on despite what is beautiful,
Life goes on despite what you love,
Life passes by the moments we wish would last forever,
There's so much that we wish could stay,
There's so much that we wish we could say,
We wish that our lives would be okay,
We just want to be okay,
We just want to enjoy the love,
We miss what has just passed,
Split seconds split within seconds,
Days fly by faster than we can absorb the memory.

We're afraid to forget as they help aid the pain,
These somber reflections... we know the stories,
They combine through time and become nonlinear,
We just begin to see memories as flashes overlaid.

All Sides

I can't choose between the two halves of myself.

One side wants to provide for the family,
One side wants to provide for myself,
The internal battle that keeps me from doing neither.

I've been going through the constant cycles,
Round and round I've been spinning since childhood,
The burden of financial struggles keeps me on the ride,
The gray floor brings horror,
It has stayed with me into adulthood,
The patterns, mindset, and desperation,
Ingrained within my psyche that leaves me chained,
I want to get off,
Get out of this sinking hole,
I want to bury it all in my past forever,
I've learned enough lessons,
Only so many times can I struggle with the same issues,
I need to rewire and learn better for myself,
Understand beyond what I've been taught,
One day come back and showcase that it was worth all I fought.

One side loves being the nucleus of the family,
One side wants to make myself the nucleus of the universe,
One side causes the shattering of the family,
One side causes me to want to leave the universe for good.

The two halves of myself,
All sides of me are me,
I just have to choose the real me.

Drifted Away

I drifted in the waters and had to make a decision,
I didn't want to get left behind,
Nor did I think I'd make the right choice,
I'd long forgotten how to use my voice,
Books lifted me above the water,
I wanted to learn, but life had real lessons for me,
I was looking for purpose blinded by the waves in front of me,
These dark tunnels led me where I was destined to go,
It took me away from my family,
It was meant to be that I spend a few years lonely,
The craft is there to master,
The city I was destined for was always above me,
I had been drowning for so long before I reached the surface.

The lights drew me here,
The telescreen told me that greatness cooked here,
I dreamed of achieving what my idols have,
There was a burning desire inside of me,
The passion boiled within to reach the top,
I had to choose...
Art or family?

My heart couldn't handle that answer,
I knew what I wanted,
But that was before I understood,
That standing for myself...
My family would understand my vision once it's in fruition,
That the seeds of my labor would grow after preparation,
That having it all was the destination.

Liquid Daydream

The tears flow slowly,
The beauty of what was and what will be,
The recollection of moments secrete nectar,
That gives joy and love,
The charm that nostalgia brings,
A smile that rises from beneath the surface.

The years fly by fast,
What bloomed has long ago withered,
The loveliness of the fast life,
The excitement that oozes within,
Brings an allure for an endless amount,
The blessings of glamor that come after the valor.

Time passes by and never says bye,
Before we know it,
It's gone and we pray it returns,
Photography freezes time,
As words do with stories,
The internet creates forever.

We try and compute emotions,
That leave us missing what used to be,
The screens allow us to be seen,
The screens extract the soul of what we are,
Everything happens so rapidly,
We become vapid,
We lose what makes us human.

Living Graphics

The older I get,
The less sure I am about anything,
The more I unlearn everything I've been taught,
The more I realize I never knew anything,
The past isn't what we've been taught,
The past isn't what I remember,
Fictional pictures as these are fictional scriptures,
From what I think I remember,
Things I created,
Things I saw through my filter of what I've lived,
The irony in that,
I only know as much as I know at that point,
Therefore, what is real when my senses only feel?
What they think is certain,
What they think is pain,
What receptors tell my brain is that thing,
Neural programming in this digital program,
What is real when we're programmed to feel?
If a wise man knows nothing,
Why are we expected to know everything?
Why are we playing this game of life — that's a game?
Living videos rendering the possibilities,
Processing the information oftentimes with no definite intention.

Lost in the reality of it,
Lost in the simulation of it all,
Lost in the world that isn't certain,
Lost without purpose,
Lost in the memories.

There Will Be Tears

A bliss that I forever miss,
Falling asleep and waking up in your own bed,
Unaware of how you got there,
While still feeling on your forehead — your mother's kiss,
The simplicity of that memory that comes to me,
The heaven it was to feel no responsibility,
What I took for granted,
As everything to me was handed,
As a kid loving the wild and carefree,
Parents did everything for me,
Until there was a blink of an eye that happened too fast,
Too fast I was given the duty to take care of myself,
I was the oldest with authority,
I will take care of my siblings just as I promised my parents,
That burden fell onto me, and I carried it elegantly,
The man of the house while my dad was at work,
I disciplined them to make sure they knew the reality,
But I never expected reality to hit me so hard.

As I grew older, the burden became heavier,
It was no longer protect the house,
It was establishing your own home and family,
All while I strove to get my parents their dream home,
And take care of my entire family,
That became heavy on my conscious as I failed to set a foundation,
Time after time, I suffered and it all fell apart,
To the point where my family started falling apart,
I cried as that fell on me,
A part of me died as that fell on me,
The blame was placed on me,
The crybaby of the family,
I have to expect the responsibility and accept the accountability,
A misfortune for many to bear the weight,
But I will not allow my misses to keep me from winning,
Until I obtain the fortune for my family,
I will prosper beyond my own limitations,
As I see the invisible and turn it into the tangible,
Until I see my parent's hopes of me become real and I see them smiling,
There will be happy tears after years of suffering.

Runaway

Why do I keep running from myself?

There's a lot going through my mind,
It seems like I'm afraid of my own success,
How can I be more afraid of that than failure?
There's a lot going on in this mind of mine,
And it seems like I've been keeping myself hostage,
Why won't I allow myself to be free?
Why don't I let myself win?
I try to do so much and I accomplish more than most,
But it seems like I run away from the congratulatory toast,
It's like I want it all but I stop myself from all that will get me there,
I want to get there,
I have to get there,
I have to let go of my own shackles,
Release myself when I have the key,
I've always had the key but I've been playing victim,
The victim as if the world was against me,
No one was, no one cared,
The only thing that kept me in chains,
Was my own brain hoping to never change beyond the same,
I was comfortable in the same,
But I couldn't allow the comfortable to drive me sane,
For insane is how you change the game.

Slips Away

There's an uncertainty in my soul,
About whether I'm worth this talent bestowed upon me,
I seem to be continually running away from myself,
I can't seem to take the burden of this craft,
The world is awaiting for me to reach my potential,
My family is waiting for me to become what I've said I would be,
The impatience boils and is unspoken,
Just faces of disappointment hidden behind their smiles,
They can't seem to tell me the truth,
But they shouldn't have to when I'm lacking truth towards myself,
They support me and my creative pursuits,
But I've yet to reach the milestones I've proclaimed,
When I don't reach them, no one says anything,
But I feel ashamed...
I can't help but feel like I've let everyone down,
I'm getting older,
The sunsets are setting faster,
My parent's mortality displays itself,
Something I can't run away from,
The torment as time slips away,
I don't have the capacity to give them what they deserve...

Yet,
But at what point does that come to fruition,
My whole life I've listened to my intuition,
It led me to life as an artist,
Threw me into a life where I had to adjust,
Telling my family to hold onto faith a little longer,
There's power in believing in myself first,
Doing everything for myself first,
That is an absolute must,
Within myself — I have to learn trust.

Golden Sun

I was so focused on searching for yellow while submerged,
Within the waters I was drowning…
So deep — the blue became black,
I failed to realize I was surrounded by yellow.

I'm about to reach the surface,
As I'm tired of the yesterdays,
Here comes me…

The Golden Son.

All you need(ed) is love.

My (love) life began on Abb(e)y Road...

Elementary / Award Ceremony

Sometimes I beg for the old times,
When I had bedtimes,
Where under covers I would read books with flashlights,
Now, I have insomnia at times,
I don't have a regular sleep schedule,
Something which my mom still gets mad about,
When there was the only worry of waking up for school,
There was so much to learn,
But to me it was elementary.

I prayed for when the TV cart rolled into class,
Then instead of daydreaming during lectures,
I got to see moving pictures,
Where words from actors moved me as books would,
I dreamed of filming my own one day,
Being surrounded by beautiful actresses,
Getting to capture their beauty with a lens,
While being scared to talk to my crush across the room,
The ease of days like those,
I couldn't wait for recess where I would excel at every sport,
But the fun of playing with friends was everything,
The innocence of cooties being our biggest fear,
When your crush would smile at you and it felt like the end was near,
The rush of excitement that made you want to run away forever,
When Valentine's Day came around…
You wanted to subtly give your crush a special card,
But that wasn't too special — so they wouldn't realize you liked them.

Oh, what a whirlwind of emotion as children,
The simplicity of life that we crave to go back to,
Recollections of award ceremonies…
As your mom took pictures of you holding a piece of paper,
As I sit here older looking back at the old times,
Just wanting to make my parents proud,
Where I can capture pictures with words and shift paradigms,
Although, I no longer have bedtimes,
I aspire for the feeling of her smiling…
As I hand over my awards and lots of paper,
I'll make sure I don't sleep nor stop daydreaming until I do.

Reruns of Memories

These dreams seem so far-fetched to others,
They can't grasp my tendencies,
They can't even predict my next move,
I've believed in myself,
There was a time I lost myself,
But I recouped my self-esteem,
While others never even dreamed,
I knew life isn't want it seems because I could control it with my mind,
There were levels that I obtained with thoughts,
There were thoughts that kept me winded,
There were moments that I wanted it all,
I choose the freedom to dream,
I choose to dream because so many stop — dreaming.

So many get stuck reminiscing,
So many end up doing nothing,
So many end up choosing the safe choice,
They stay where they are because it's all they know,
There's no other thing to look forward to,
The past is something they think about till time passes,
They focus on the things they've already done,
They get stuck glorifying the things they've done,
They never do anything more than what they've done,
They're done with life without being aware of it,
They die before they've known they're dead,
They repeat the memories in their head,
They recapture images as they lay on their bed,
Reruns of their past fun, this leaves them running in place,
Never seeing that there's more to life than highlights,
They can't grasp that there's life beyond the comfortable,
Anything beyond that to them seems like a fable,
They peaked early in their life and attached themselves to that image,
They can't seem to go beyond their own limitations,
The sensations they've never felt and hardships they've never dealt with,
The deep love they've never experienced that is heartfelt,
They can't take the fire of passion,
They can't let their ego and memories melt,
Because that requires growth and letting go.

To settle is to die early.

The melancholy from the constant memory of who I used to be.

The essence of the old me.

Nostalgia is nothing but joy tinged with sadness.

Fell in Love...

Those that loved me no longer feel that way,
I'm left alone without much to say,
I've lost all my purpose,
I'm crying every day,
Tendencies of those that lack masculinity,
I was left a shell of a man,
I didn't know how to be one.

The girl I loved stayed secretly looking for one,
She entertained others while I was suicidal,
I just wanted loyalty and to be loved by her,
The girl I loved flaunted her attention from guys,
At the beach, I begged her to save me from my dark thoughts,
She looked at me in disgust and proceeded to break my trust.

I'm left stopped on the bridge,
The bay whispered my name seductively,
It sounded so lovely that I wanted to fall,
At least that made me feel something I hadn't,
The bay made me feel wanted,
I saw myself reflecting on the water,
I fell in love with the thought of jumping...
Into a relationship with (the) bay,
It'd keep me afloat after a life of drowning,
Just wasn't sure I'd survive the impact,
I've become fragile,
The bay would be hard at first,
I could break its thin layer,
Bay keeps waving at me,
It's welcoming me into her waters.

//

The car idles on the bridge,
Flashes of memories and baggage,
Living this life damaged where it'd all be solved with a second of courage,
The bay would take my breath away before I hit,
Diving in — I could brag that I hit… it nicely,
No other car in sight gave me the advantage,
No one could stop me,
The only person getting in the way was me,
No one cares about degrees — floating upside down,
What better way than in my hometown,
The landmark where I mark my legacy as I land,
Or lack of legacy because I haven't done anything worth telling,
A failed storyteller who lived without much of a story to tell,
Whose writing washed with waves of the bay,
Dreams unfulfilled that drown me already,
The self-pressure to achieve it all in my twenties,
To have it all figured out and erase all doubt,
Seconds were passing and I was second-guessing my choice,
Lack of vision lead me to this point which sparked a vision,
I saw drops that weren't water… but tears from my family,
The devastation of my absence destroyed my mother,
All that my father sacrificed for me had gone to waste,
My brothers were left without an older brother they see as an idol,
I came back to earth as my car idles on the bridge,
I was drowning on the bridge and no one was aware,
I felt no one genuinely cared and I was a waste of life,
I had to acknowledge that I mattered and encouraged myself to live,
Thank God I was indecisive,
A creative mind can sometimes be destructive,
I'm far from living with a positive outlook,
But sometimes I look out over the bridge…
And smile that I still have the choice.

Far Away

I chose to put myself first and leave my family,
I moved towards something greater and a new city,
As a child, I knew I wanted more and to leave a legacy,
Nauseous of the future but I must live beyond the cautious,
I've built a ship to travel through the waters of doubt,
The gray fog consumes the sky and doesn't allow me to see...
I've become sick,
Homesick.

Sinister Sadness

When I've cut everyone off,
Am I even welcome?

How could I return home?

Will they accept me with open arms?
Or shield themselves because of the wounds I caused...

Hiding suicidal thoughts from them all,
I needed escape from the ones that loved me most,
How could they love me, someone so ugly?
I never deserved any of their care or affinity,
Alone in the world, I felt crazy,
No one saw me.

Going through the grief of who I used to be,
I didn't recognize myself — I hated looking at me,
I became obese,
As the mirror brought internal horror,
How could anyone even love a piece of me?
I hated myself.

I figured I was doing them a favor,
By choosing to release myself from their lives,
It didn't matter if it was friends or relatives,
No mercy as I cut everyone off.

I was consumed by the vile which inspired my own exile,
I thought to myself, my life was never worthwhile,
As I waited for the scythe's arrival.

Best Days

I've gotten stuck in a loop within my mind,
Repeating past mistakes in my head,
Insomnia keeps my eyes open at night,
Thinking that I've lived my best days,
They're all behind me and none more are coming,
Life becomes a series of horrible nights,
The darkness surrounds every aspect of me,
My best days are behind me,
Ones where I wasn't as lonely,
I could feel the love from friends and family,
What if I've run out of good days?
I got them early and now I'm left empty...

Empty of days that make me feel happy,
The sorrow consumes my every tomorrow.

Fiending for a feeling, I ask those if there's any joy I could borrow,
Knowing I'm broke so I can't repay them,
I take and take because a smile I can no longer fake,
Maybe my life was a mistake,
The sadness overflows every part of my body,
The achievements of everyone around overshadow mine,
No need to get my hopes up because it was an easy foreshadow,
Hoping I could forgo this life,
Where I've so long suffered this gruesome limbo,
Where it feels as if death was coming in slow,
There's nothing intoxicating about living life,
I wonder if the bottle will help throttle the funeral,
A fate that brings the fatal sooner than later,
No use in being hopeful when I'm feeling mournful,
Living with the death of my best days,
Hurried to be buried were those days,
Where every birthday you'd wish for death,
The yesterdays outweigh any possible future days,
The years only brought more tears,
No faith in my future getting better...

Wait... There possibly was one more day for me,
My last best day could be me leaving earth forever.

Smile

The torture that you suffer through,
One that no one else sees,
One that you cover up so nicely,
One that you hide behind a painted smile.

It's been a while since I last saw you,
I can't believe at one point I thought about killing you,
You used to be so kind despite the deep depression that you had,
One that was an agony to go through,
One that made everyone around you disappear,
One that made you cut ties with those that love you,
I remember you,
It's been a while,
I hated you.

You were so lost and confused,
Mentally abused yourself,
Despised yourself,
Your self was never yourself.

You lost your sanity at one point,
You tried to escape within poetry,
Ironically, those ideas you wrote about left you lonelier,
They saw you as crazy and distanced themselves slowly,
How pathetic of you to tie yourself so strongly to people that never cared,
They only cared about the value and knowledge you brought to them,
They never cared about anything you did,
So, you ran away and hid,
For years, blankets full of tears,
Subconscious — full of fears,
A disgrace, you could never face yourself.

Now, I just read your words,
I look at old pictures of you,
Shake my head in disgust,
Then I look up at the mirror,
And see a photocopy.

The dangers of being alone,
The fear of being alone,
Prone to the alone for dark thoughts,
Prone to the alone for pure thoughts,
To act in love is seen as devilish,
"How could you act so selfless? Focus on yourself."
All I want for others is joy,
The constant belittling eats me alive,
The constant separation of those I love,
They used to love me, but now they don't,
They used to want to be around,
Till they found out my inner thoughts,
The high-pitched sound of truth they can't handle,
I become someone they can't handle,
Out of their control,
The imprisonment of a social circle,
Step away and you're sent away,
The betrayal is nothing to them,
The realization that you're nothing to them,
What you thought was love,
What you thought was trust,
What you thought was genuine,
Was all in...
Your head,
For once what they don't believe is said,
To them, you're better off dead.

I feel like that,
Maybe I am better off dead,
I feel like that...
All the time.

No rhyme.

I'm afraid of the changes that are occurring so rapidly,
I'm trying to tie myself to the past moments,
Only to realize its noose is leading to my death.

Sleepy and Hollow

The alarm clock blares loudly enough to awaken the whole house,
I don't hear a sound as I lay sound asleep,
One of my parents barges in yelling,
"¡Despiértate ya!"
The sudden jolt causes me to get out of bed.

These reminders in my head of days that I was depressed,
My life was unworthy so I slept my life away,
In reality, I was useless so I slept,
Sleeping was the only moment that I felt happy,
They were the only times I liked life,
I hated my life but I didn't want it to end,
Because that means I could no longer dream,
Which was the best part of life,
I was unmotivated and had nothing going for me,
My bed was the only place that I felt safe,
Being in bed allowed me to be lazy,
I would sleep half the day on my favorite days,
That's what caused so much turmoil in the soil of my family,
Once the motivation and inspiration of the family,
I became the demonstration of what not to be,
The letdowns as I let everyone down,
It made me want to escape the world and sleep even more.

...

...

In the hours awake, I would pretend to stay busy,
I did nothing, to lay in bed was my comfort,
All I got was pity from my family,
Maybe, I secretly craved that someone would care,
That someone would come and save me,
But even if they did, I'd lash out back at them...
The darkness under blankets was the only thing that understood me,
It loved me more than anything,
No one cared what I was doing while I slept,
No one asked questions of my future or purpose while I slept,
The burnout of outside pressures to prosper,
The night owl in me came alive at night,
But the "normal" never suited me as I slept during the day,
The hostility that would cause between me and my parents,
I could never wake up when the alarms went off,
Snooze after snooze, I didn't want to wake up,
I'd rather stay in bed and live there, I enjoyed the comfort,
They want me to be over sleep, all I love to do is oversleep,
Sleep is the only thing that made me happy,
And everyone's tried to take it away from me.

When?

When will it end?
When will this pain stop?
When will my life just mend?
I'm tired of this constant weight,
This weight on my mind,
When will the pressure stop?
This burden buries me more each second,
Hardships drowning my psyche,
Strength on the exterior,
The interior on the verge of shattering,
Struggling to make something of myself,
Struggling to make myself proud,
I've been gaining weight,
I've been gaining hate,
This weight of hate towards myself,
It may be too late,
I'm tired of this constant pondering,
When will my life end?
Maybe then, the pain will stop.

Rest in the Light

You crossed my mind,
We haven't talked in years,
I hope you're well.

I just heard the news...
You're no longer here.

It pains me that you'd just disappear,
That you probably weren't thinking clear,
Escaped, left us all in the dark,
Escaped, you released yourself from the dark,
I pray you found light in your final moments,
That you are surrounded by light after your final breath,
It's saddening how much you would suffer,
All of us unaware of the agonizing torment,
You spent every waking moment feeling.

I can't begin to understand how you felt,
Nor judge how you dealt with the torture,
The weight of your death has tied me to depression,
I'm unsure of how to grieve in a world without you,
The world has been a bit more gloomy since you left,
Left with a wound that bleeds for you,
The replays of memories still make me smile,
Your energy that brought many so much joy...
Will be missed more than anything,
To your family — you were everything,
Even if you never saw it as real,
I hope now that you're resting... you are able to heal,
I have to accept that you're gone,
I have to carry on,
I hope we meet again,
As I rest in broken pieces without you,
I pray you rest in peace.

Close Call

A brief moment and it's all gone,
Your family gone in an instant,
Instantly, the gruesome pain that comes with chains,
That will be strapped to my body and mind for life,
Where everything is attached to them,
Where everything I do becomes in honor of them,
What a dark place to live,
What a dark place I'm living in, I can't imagine worse,
These chains reign my ambitions,
The rain pours and brings horrors,
There's not a thing I could do that could change the reality,
No poem, no writing at all that could bring you back.

What joy you brought to this reality,
What unity you brought whenever you were around,
Now, you're bound to another realm,
Where you'll be forever missed,
Where once the earth with you, it was blessed,
Where the agony sits in place,
To face the torture from the loss of pure.

I love my family,
I love every single one of them,
To lose one brings communal agony,
Imagine multiple in one swing,
The craziness of one thing,
Of one instant,
Thankful that life continues,
Glimpses of death show us fragility,
Where we become aware of our moment's ability of death,
Solely for the reason to give us agility,
Life isn't meant for stability,
It gives us doses, sneak peeks into neurosis,
To remind us to appreciate the moments of current bliss,
Before it's something we forever miss.

Callings

This relentless thought within my head,
"Save them, save them, they need you to save them."

The thought keeps me awake at night,
With no end of the suffering in sight,
Ridiculed for not making the right decisions,
Yet I'm seen as the savior because of my visions.

I have to cut ties,
Maybe not forever but temporarily,
I need separation from this temptation,
It's in my blood and heart to care for others,
But that stops me from caring about myself.

I'll never be able to see what lies ahead,
When I'm so focused on what I left behind.

The Pains of Growing

Before I knew reality was pixels or had to worry about radar guns,
Before I put words together to make new ones.

The two artists of the family,
One held a guitar while the other drew,
My love of music and animation began there.

Fifteen years later from my birth...
How much I wanted to be like both of you,
I looked up to you,
That's why you stayed so high,
I wanted so much to be like you,
An aluminum can destroyed my innocence,
You both inspired the fire,
I wanted to fit in with you both,
To get high like you guys,
I figured you'd catch me in the clouds,
Instead, the sirens blared loudly,
The panic set in and I thought the world was ending,
Instead of helping me... the party continued,
So, I locked myself in the car.

Who would've known a car was the only thing that made me feel safe,
I was sitting passenger, alone in the car,
My mind was calling for help,
The death of my innocence,
I wanted to be so much like you both...
That I let you betray my trust,
My role models left me alone in some random car model,
I had trouble catching my breath,
The death of my innocence.

...

...

The car is the only place I felt safe,
I became a chauffeur for others,
Carrying them to their dreams,
Mapping out points A to B,
I was so lost that I was mindlessly drifting,
Driving on roads that weren't meant for me,
Because I forgot about the inner child in me.

I carried shame, hid that from everyone my whole life,
I wanted to be perfect — create realities without leaves,
Now, I'm letting go and leaving all the resentment behind.

Some people aren't meant to be role models,
But as you grow up you understand...
Their role was in modeling what not to do,
As they were running away from their potential and themselves,
Trying to coast through life without directions,
They were trippin' in circles.

I detached and took a tour by myself,
So I could be better and discover myself,
They certainly taught me lessons from their mistakes,
That was the test to mature, gain my drive, and stay on track,
That's the one thing I passed... in a circle.

Single-Player Game

We used to be the best of friends,
We knew each other's darkest secrets,
Those countless hours playing with toys,
We created stories, whole movies,
Action figures became actors,
We would wrestle for invisible belts,
Before we felt the daunting pressure to find answers,
So close, you'd think we were brothers,
We practically grew that way,
We bonded over everything,
We took on life like a two-player game,
Each of us with a controller but a set objective,
Take over the world together,
We shared the same last name,
Let's share the glory at the top,
I care(d) so deeply about you,
But as life went on, it felt one-sided,
Until, finally, we grew away from each other,
To this day, I never knew why,
Was it envy?
Competition that turned unfriendly?
Did life carry us towards different paths?
I thought we were family... but I guess that never mattered to you,
Did friends mean more than our unity?
Maybe it's on me for having expectations you could never meet,
Maybe we were always opposite...
Until that attracted us to separate poles of the earth,
I chose a life of risk, you chose one of safety,
From sharing bunk beds to butting heads,
I often think about how you're doing lately,
I always wanted to make you proud, I looked up to you,
But I guess, that made it fact that you looked down on me,
I want to see you become great and win,
I love you, cousin.

Seems like you're doing everything by the book,
While here I am writing books,
I wish I had written a different ending to our story,
But not all of them end happily.

The Sister I Never Had

As the internet rose in my world,
My space diminished,
And faces were no longer in books but on screens,
We loved to talk, share secrets and life stories,
What a zeitgeist that made us cry,
After the doom of the financial crisis,
Who would've thought we'd one day share a room,
Then, we shared a high school,
You took me in and introduced me to your friends,
Fun times, drunk times,
Crazy how your friend(s) fell in love with me,
Who would've imagined that reality,
Crazy that it bred an almost jealousy,
That was always weird to me,
Which led to secrecy,
That started the fall of our relationship as family,
Sometimes I regret even going there,
Dating your friends led to a lot of hurt,
Most importantly, it ruined our bond,
Your insecurity bled into my girlfriends,
Where the wounds were irreparable,
Your mental became unstable,
Which lead you to some questionable decisions,
It all went up in smoke,
Ironically, you were willing to destroy us,
While staying friends with them,
That's when I learned there's no loyalty...
From women,
And even amongst family.

Like a sister I never had,
I'm glad I only had brothers.

What is Love?

You wanted to learn love from a heartbroken man,
A budding flower desperate for nourishment,
You were looking for a light,
Unaware of what love is since your parents split at an early age,
Different worlds that came together,
Altering the worlds we were living,
You had to fight to survive,
While I was fighting to survive love,
The shattering that I experienced was drastic,
What looked like true love from the outside,
Was rotting within until I broke free against my will,
When she broke up with me,
You were full of wonder and questions,
I loved to answer the poetic nature of it all,
What I was trying to run away from,
You wanted to run towards,
You were so void of feeling emotion,
When I couldn't handle feeling so much of it,
I wasn't aware that I was leading you towards pain,
A life only beautiful in theory,
The purest of love is only ever felt once,
You were tired of girls that only wanted the temporary,
I admired you could pull women of all sorts with ease,
But you only wanted to hold one,
We tried to teach other lessons but I never let my fear go,
You wanted the Spider-Man love with Mary Jane,
I was trying to catch as many as I could through the web,
You eventually did catch her and you got a taste of love,
Something that you kept running back to,
Even at the cost of you.

...

...

I couldn't blame you because emotions can make you do stupid things,
It can have you returning to what isn't good for you,
Even if it's just for the temporary highs,
That devotion can stagnate your motion,
Sometimes it leads to the separation of those you love,
Trust me, I know...
I wish you would've asked me that question,
Maybe you would've listened,
I just wish it would've gotten through to you,
Because when she leaves...
And your heart is set ablaze,
The last thing you want when you're heartbroken and fiending,
Is to be without the family that has been there since the beginning.

Book(s) of Genesis

I was stripped of my hometown,
We learned to live together,
Rarely talked to each other,
We were in our own worlds,
I was in a new city but digitally living back home,
I couldn't let go,
Through screens, I stayed close to friends I left back home,
Your family took us in when we had nothing,
We took a risk because what we'd always done had failed,
We slowly built the foundation of what would come in the future,
I gave you long-winded life lessons,
As I attempted to break you out of your shell.

From afar aligned the stars...
We became closer than ever,
The world we created,
It was miraculous,
It was us against the evil in the world,
Traveling the country,
Planting seeds that vibrate positivity,
The world was burning and we chose to battle it with frost,
Soon, the fire of life we had... got cold,
As the time passed and we were met with responsibility,
We created so much good with our intentions,
The ability to manifest became elementary,
Then, we lost ourselves to the pressures post-graduation,
Where we were fed with fear and hesitation,
Lost our spark and oneness with the universe,
Oh, how I miss the world we created...

...

...

We allowed the world to turn us into what we hated,
The vibrancy was taken away from us,
The belief in magic was taken away from us,
The hardships hardened us,
But our ability to write was something we could trust in,
A beloved cousin that became a brother,
We helped each other, challenged each other,
To find our voice and express our suffering,
Soon after, our failures turned into wins,
What we'd so long dreamed of — we manifested,
Our connection and success was coded,
I can't help but reminisce about the world we created,
Aloneness and shame turned into poetry,
Amongst the inferno of the city,
We discovered our genesis.

Ships Sailed

I've been wondering how you've been,
You cross my mind from time to time,
I miss the laughs and sleepovers we used to have,
The gas station runs to load up on snacks,
I grew to love your family like it was my own,
Your parents raised me as if I were their own,
They kept me fed after school or on the weekends,
They gave me rides home when I was stranded,
I would be grateful for each moment,
I've been wondering where you've been,
It's been years since we've talked,
It's sad that I didn't know the last time we talked...
Would be the last time we talked,
I've tried to reach out at times,
Often left awaiting a response from a ghost,
You used to be my best friend,
We were inseparable,
Now, it's like it never existed,
How sorrowful that it's forgetful for you,
I suppose our friendship was never that deep,
And I was the one that stayed delusional,
I guess us fading apart was inevitable,
Did I outgrow you? Did you outgrow me?
Why can't you even give me a reason?
Eating myself alive over a friend who was always seasonal,
Deep affinity counts for nothing,
I just wish you would've said something,
So then, I'd suffer less,
Beating myself up,
Thinking it was something I did or said,
I guess I have to let it go,
When someone no longer wants you present in their lives,
Be thankful for the memories,
The immeasurable influence you had on my life.

One where you'd be part of my memoir,
But... I can only thank you from afar.

Envy Runs Deep

I cared about you,
I wanted you to win,
Every chance I had I would give you advice,
I wanted you to prosper beyond the city,
I thought we were friends,
But that changed the second that I had different thoughts,
Different thoughts than what you were told by (social) media,
Which made you see me as the devil.

I have always been different,
I was taught to think different,
Guess I bit into the wrong apple,
While you were the snake,
Didn't realize that's who you were,
Your layers shed quick — pieces of your disguise trailed behind you,
Fooled by my own goodness,
My own need to see everyone win,
Surrounded by hopeless sin,
And so-called friends who hate themselves within,
The envy ran deep,
As the poison from your fangs seeped into my skin,
I knew my death was coming soon,
Not literal but spiritual,
I saw who you really were,
I lost who I was,
For after that moment I never trusted the same,
Reserved and kept to myself,
Stopped giving others advice and help,
The part of me that loved to help died,
Fake friends caused the end,
The end of that version of me,
They crushed my morale,
They won until I realized...
It was done for the purpose of not elevating further than them,
They were too tied to their own friends' thoughts to think for themselves,
No wonder they exiled whoever did so,
They didn't hate me,
They hated their lack of individuality.

Care Less

Memory lane drives me insane,
There's so much pain from trying to stay the same,
I miss my old friends,
I miss getting drunk with them,
I miss laughing with them,
When we didn't care about how much we made,
When nothing mattered — we just had fun,
When there were no responsibilities,
We just had fun,
I miss those times,
The high school level drama is something I miss,
Better than the pressures of having it figured out in your early 20's,
I miss my old friends that no longer talk to me,
Sometimes, I'm not even sure why,
They just decided to separate themselves from me,
They refuse to talk to me,
I cared about them so deeply,
But whether it's my controversial thoughts...
Or no longer do they want anything to do with me,
I'm not sure,
I get too attached to the good times that I spent with them,
But people in your life come in chapters,
And they weren't meant to be in my next book,
I miss them but they don't miss me,
And I have to accept that they could care less about me,
It makes me equally angry and sad,
But I have to accept it for what it is,
Just show them they missed out on my success,
No hard feelings and accept the process of life,
Show them that everything is possible,
Even if they lose access to me as I rise up in success,
From afar I think about them as I reach stardom,
I suppress my agony that they no longer care about me.

Slow Lie

It's always the ones talking about forever that change the most rapidly,
And end up making being together — temporary.

I'm running out of love,
I've given the best of myself to those I thought were true,
Lovers, friends, and family,
That took advantage of me,
My genuine care that I gave without any left to spare,
But loyalty never existed to them,
For without that there's nothing to be had,
For without trust a relationship ceases to exist,
All that effort on my part...
And once we parted,
It was like I ceased to exist.

These slow lies,
These false apologies,
The forced attempts at rekindling,
A waste of time,
A waste of rhymes,
There was never any love on their part,
Running out of time,
Running out of love,
Running out of words,
After putting this pain again and again...
In my art.

Alone for the Lows

How do you outgrow someone that you love with all your heart?
With memories that go beyond any other person on earth,
The past with you still makes me smile,
Moments we shared still make me laugh,
But they all have passed,
They were so good that they weren't meant to last,
Over time I became an outcast,
Feeling like I had no one to talk to,
My once close friend,
Disappeared faster than I feared,
The lengths we used to go together,
Just for it all to go to waste,
Erased as if we'd never met before,
Emotions of missing you placed to the side,
Easier to hide the truth than expose emotions.

Friends become foes,
Shared highs, alone for the lows,
They carry secrets of yours,
That you can't help but fear they'll disclose out of spite,
Life without them doesn't feel right,
But you're all you have left,
Dreams to accomplish for yourself,
Maybe once you reach those lengths,
You can come back and try to make amends,
Hopefully, by then, the rekindling isn't just for pretend,
Because they can barely make ends meet,
And I have met all ends,
Where we can go back to truly being friends,
As if no time has passed at all,
Where together, we finally stand tall.

Heal

Forgiveness leaves us without stress,
When we learn to let go of the wound,
It heals itself,
But it takes us expressing our thoughts,
To feel the healing of grief.

The denial I run from comes to a halt,
It angers me that I've wasted so much time,
What if... I could bargain my way out of pain?
This depression I can't let win,
I was forced to learn from the actions of others and find acceptance.

The peace came from the pieces,
I was broken and numb but after came the wisdom,
Tiresome was rock bottom playing the victim,
I had to become what at my darkest I couldn't even fathom,
"Don't take anything personally," repeated in my mind constantly,
For what others do is a projection of their own reality,
They used me as a wall then stonewalled,
I forgave myself for allowing them access to my core,
I forgave them so I could finally soar,
Where the wounds don't torture me anymore.

The performative is often addictive,
As the crowd applauds the antics,
The drama increases profits,
You love the show — the high goes up with the digits,
Just as the points of a star want you to be,
Five bullet points of what makes a superstar,
You got a dime that pleases all five senses,
You're running out of minutes.

The fear you'll lose your magic,
The talent and why they love you,
You've lost sight and are unaware of what comes next for you,
Everything you touched turned to gold,
Your taste is what got you there in the first place,
Now, you can't handle the sound of the boos,
The audience smells the rotten before it comes out of the kitchen,
You're left without much sense as dollars and cents diminish,
You feel as though you're not finished,
But who's to say that you aren't?
Isn't an audience the point of creation?
What happens when they expose the fabrication?
Was your career even worth the nominations and top five lists?
Was it worth being called one of this generation's prophets?

When do you realize that the artist is never free?
You're tied to the chains of public perception,
An open-air prison where you're fed validation,
Starving for it as that's the only reason for your creations,
Preferring glass walls so they can see and pity you,
Your life source becomes the product placements you endorse,
As you're left with remorse and you're paid to reinforce the agenda,
All for the sake of a comma.

Soon, the music stops and the cheers silence,
Your mind becomes a haunting acapella,
You and your fans trapped in the nostalgia,
You lost your mind and became a hollow replica,
The five fingers of your hand reach for what's metal and takes shots,
But it's not what you picture it to be,
You count backwards from three,
This is what it comes down to...
One bullet point left before the end of your career,
The final joke as you end with a BANG!

The true jesters do oft create profits.

While the painted jesters do oft prove prophets.

Bravo, Mexican Shakespeare.

Mi Tierra

¿Cómo podría expresar el amor que siento por este país?
Aquí nacieron mis padres en un estado de tierra fértil,
Y las mujeres más hermosas del mundo,
Donde varias generaciones se han unido...
Con mucho amor, formando una gran familia.

Aunque a veces me dormía en el camino,
Recuerdo con nostalgia esos viajes en auto de 16 horas,
Con la emoción de llegar y ver a la familia,
Comer mariscos, tacos, dulces mexicanos y tirar cohetes,
Las tortillas hechas a mano por mi abuela eran una bendición,
A mi abuelo le encantaba bromear,
Nos tiraba gotitas de café caliente con su cuchara,
Y decía que eran los moscos,
Le gustaba pasearnos en la hamaca,
Que el mismo tejió mientras nos arrullaba con su canto.

Las fiestas de cumpleaños fueron especiales donde conocí buenos amigos,
Las Navidades eran con música, la alegría de la banda,
Tantos primos, tíos y sobrinos que parecía un ejército,
Había bastante comida y alcohol para alimentar a todo un pueblo,
Semana Santa era la playa,
Acampar todos juntos, bañarnos, jugar en la arena, lotería,
Contábamos anécdotas y chistes donde las risas eran interminables.

Mi familia viene de un pueblo humilde,
Pero grande en valores, amor y unión familiar,
Mis padres vinieron aquí por una vida mejor,
Un abuelo era pescador y otro empresario,
Tengo que construirme un barco en un nuevo mar,
Tengo que cimentarme como empresario,
Honrando a mis abuelos y prosperar en Estados Unidos,
Es mi destino que mi familia se sienta orgullosa — enaltecer el apellido,
No necesariamente ser famoso,
Solamente hacer que su sacrificio al cambiar de país y dejar sus raíces...
Valió la pena,
Agradezco a Dios por mi tierra,
Que aunque no nací ahí, soy parte de ella,
Por eso y por mucho más estoy agradecido y orgulloso de ser de Sinaloa.

High Stakes

Do I stay in the past and remember the good times?
Stay there attempting to recreate them for my sanity?
Or do I want to drive to the freeway...
Where I can be free in ways I never imagined?

The freeway is dangerous I've been told,
I've been told to stay off of it my whole life,
As if I was committing suicide,
Praying they were wrong as I take this ride...

There comes a fork in the road,
That leaves me insatiable,
I was born with a hunger for greatness,
I couldn't leave myself to stay lifting plates from tables,
When I could be the one sitting as plates are placed,
I knew what was at stake...
I had to make a decision against the norm,
Leave the comfortable despite being unpolished,
A ma(e)stro as I orchestrate these words within people's minds,
A man dedicated to the craft,
I create waves with my artistry as I stare at the ocean,
Far away from my prime...
Because I haven't even fully tapped into my mind,
I was designed by the divine,
To shine and make my bloodline proud,
Even if they don't agree with me currently,
They'll see the magic manifested in our reality,
And smile at the fact I overcame all the limitations,
And my life becomes a demonstration for fearless decisions,
As ancestors were my guardians, I just had to believe in myself,
They were guiding me despite my current family creating resistance,
They want me to beat all restrictions to inspire generations to come,
I'm enhancing my circumstance so I can advance,
I took a stance against my family and took a chance...
That allowed the exit of the freeway to also be the entrance.

The choice lingers within my psyche constantly,
Follow the path given by society...
Or chase the dream of writing poetry.

The safe choice kills you slowly,
The dream leaves constant uncertainty.

The safe choice makes your parents happy,
The dream causes beautiful insanity.

The safe choice gets you robotic praise,
The dream is fulfilling but you get called crazy.

The safe choice is something no one dreams about,
The dream is a dangerous choice to those that think safe.

The choice to be safe keeps you imprisoned,
The choice to follow dreams leaves you isolated.

Is the choice to be lonely, better than safety?
What's scarier than suppressing your own potential?

Fearful of the future is no way to live.

Better to turn dreams into reality,
Where to you — it always was the safe choice.

I bet on myself.

I was the only one left on the boat.

When I realized I was in my own race...

That's when the powerful ruler who knows the Gods showed himself.

He taught me his trade and mindset.

That allowed me to truly believe in myself.

I hated my gut — once I started trusting it...

That is when the weight of the failure vanished.

I've spent so much of my life within a car.

You can't stay parked and expect to move.

You can't stay idle and expect to become an idol.

All it takes is the courage to take action.

That is where drive comes from.

Scenic Route

My drive takes me to roads unexplored,
I blink and seem to have traveled miles ahead of everyone else,
I don't recall the journey much,
The blur of this tour towards greatness,
I can't help but look in the rearview from time to time,
I've gone so far beyond my past,
Where is everyone else that grew up with me?
Was there a moment that separated me from them?
Or was I meant to surpass them all?
Did I just happen to have the right fuel for this journey?
What happened to those that rode passenger?

Everything happened so fast,
There was no race against any other person but my past self,
Maybe that's why I feel so nostalgic,
Every mile I lost a part of me...
I couldn't help but look straight the whole way,
I wanted more for myself, more than most ever did,
This road leads me beyond my own capabilities.

I'm opening doors for these opportunities,
Seems like I'm in my own lane,
The lane has my name on it,
All this was destined for me,
Where I only focus on me,
Breaking personal records,
Checking no one else's record but understanding I'm the best,
I've had it in me,
All it took was flooring the pedal,
I was always able to conquer this artful battle,
Grateful I took a gamble on myself,
Accepting that I was abnormal from the rest,
Meant for colossal success,
This ride where I found joy,
Where life is finally colorful.

Nostos.
Algos.

I don't want to return,
To the suffering.

When nostalgia eats you alive,
You long to starve before it consumes your life,
Learning that it's more detrimental than helpful,
You must release yourself from the chokehold,
The lessons taught at the time are worth gold,
Once you release yourself...
Watch the manifestations unfold.

There's a certain hurt we feel when memories resurface,
A pain we choose to not face.

We tend to forget what makes us happy,
There isn't a scar that reminds us of our happiness,
Yet... we learn so little from peace.

I stripped myself away from those I love,
They returned the energy — an unspoken feud,
I was left in the darkness of solitude,
It destroyed me until there was nothing of my identity left,
I felt as though, I couldn't continue,
I had no one to impress, no audience,
Something I overvalued as my perception was skewed,
As if I had died, I was irrelevant on earth,
A life without a platform,
There was no need to perform.

This isolation hardened me,
The quiet lightened me.

I'd finally given myself the praise that I so direly craved.

The only expression of self was towards myself.

I was completely free.

The "E" Show

Ladies and gentlemen...
Let me take you back to '93,
Where Erik was born before he'd ever heard a multi-platinum-selling CD,
Then, in '02 as if almost by a divine design,
A nine-year-old was holding a jewel case,
Little did he know that there lay gold,
Compact gems within a disc,
I was far from a man but it's when I began walking,
I pressed play starting the show.

In that moment, I was singing,
I wasn't white but I lived in America,
On the first song, little Erik was spoken to,
Words projected onto the walls of my mind,
I could piece them together as I'd seen for the first time,
Brown eyes but I knew I'd never lose.

I vividly remember asking my mom, "Can I be a rapper when I grow up?"
She smiled and responded, "You can do whatever makes you happy."

I grew up and society told me to go to college,
A good job was necessary, not this dream of being an artist,
During which I grew ideas to start a business,
But the writer within me wanted to be free,
Meanwhile, my mom's yelling at me to clean out my closet,
Out of anger, I began to dance with words within square pages,
On pages is where they stayed as I released a poetry book,
All this commotion from saying women's emotions run deep as oceans,
These words became soldiers—
Taking bullets from the depression and criticism,
Once so-called family and friends turned shady,
I took on a role as **DELACRUZ**,
And began to be hated and discriminated against,
Now, I look back at the time when my motto to start as a writer was:
"Picket signs for my wicked rhymes."

...

...

I never meant to hurt anyone as I was the one hurting,
I almost lost my freedom over a female,
I learned they come and go, I can't be her Superman,
This world's too much, I've swallowed all the red pills I could,
Letting people say what they want to say,
Saying goodbye to my past self,
Escaping towards the hills of Hollywood,
This haunting echo to say goodbye to Hollywood before it consumes me,
I'm sorry Ma, if you have to explain that your son's gone crazy,
Dreams of coming from practically nothing,
To being able to have anything I ever wanted,
That's why I write for these lost kids who don't have a thing,
This show sparked a visionary, for most — the vision is scary,
As my wisdom in their eyes — pollutes and could start a revolution,
Reading the words of me spillin' my heart through this pen,
They know that I'll never be that Erik again,
I'm full of controversy and clutch up in the face of adversity,
The fire inside will never die even beyond thirty,
Where would poetry be — without me.

My genius will be written until the whole world knows,
Where by the audience roses — I'm bestowed,
As they rise and chant for an encore and I get bravos from my heroes,
Till I collapse, and these curtains close.

Chapter Three

Heart's Renaissance

Headquarters

The memories turned the darkness colorful.

Raised to find disgust in the green,
Tired of the rage — bleeding red for ones that never cared,
Fearful of the purple world, that's in the dream state.

The yellows and blues intertwine as I look for signs,
The emotions blend well,
My whole life I attempted to separate them assuming there's hate,
There was a misunderstanding,
Now... the colors are dancing,
The sadness had consumed my life for so long,
But the joy decided it was time to step up,
I overcame all my worries as I climbed up the stairs,
Overlooking all the islands I was stranded on for so long,
I watch them fall, piece by piece,
Piece by piece, I lose parts of myself,
Blacking out before they fall,
I learned to let go,
I can't fight what's inevitable,
The pieces were meant to fall in order to climb,
To feel lighter as I rise through the darkness.

I can no longer let emotions take control,
I have control of my soul to make prosperity my goal.

Inside — I'll know which door to choose,
Make a conscious decision to grab the knob,
Happiness is an inside job.

Creation of Life

Seven days,
Seven elements.

One day,
Humans were birthed,
Within the garden...
They grew to live and fend for themselves,
They learned to hunt for food and fend for their family,
They learned their purpose and continued the population,
They built communities, cities, and systems,
They sought expression and understanding of life,
They engraved thoughts and painted their lives for future generations,
The labor of six days leads to resting,
The resting led to creating where we function as the divine,
Humans turned into artists expressing the beauty of life,
The beauty which we're surrounded by all seven days,
With hopes of replicating on earth what God created in a week,
As artists understand creation isn't for the weak.

The seven elements were periodically inspired within,
To escape from the distraction of sin.

Humans drawing the line of just being hunters and gatherers,
Beginning to understand we can shape our reality through ideas,
As we form our lives and we take our drawings to the third-dimensional,
The burning desire to reach the fifth-dimensional space —
That is obtainable,
Where we ascend higher than the texture placed on objects...
We can feel with our hands,
The celestial body uprooted from its grounded values,
Transcending beyond the palette of colors earth has for us.

Beauty is what evokes the intense and pure elevation of soul,
It is not—intellectual nor inspired of the heart—rather it is the effect,
The delight, at first sight, creates the enrichment and pleasures of life.

Beauty in its simplicity is a golden ratio,
God blessing each detail with delicacy,
Perfect symmetry and harmony that is heavenly.

Mindset

I don't remember what happiness feels like,
Happiness that wasn't related to love,
I don't remember what that felt like,
I've lost a lot in my life,
I've lost more parts of me than success I've gained,
Just hoping for a breakthrough,
Monetary success beyond the temporary,
An abundance of wealth that makes it difficult to create stealth,
Being in optimal health,
I want to obtain everything,
I want everything.

Everything comes to me,
My mind creates my reality,
I already have what I want,
I tell myself that,
But I miss what happiness was,
Stuck in a mental battle,
That happiness is beyond the tangible,
It comes from within,
But within currently feels empty,
I used to want someone to complete me,
But deep down, I know I have what it takes to complete me,
I just have to search for what's necessary,
All of that is inside,
It starts with wanting to change,
Finding the beauty in the little things,
The answers are inward,
That allows me to go onward,
Beyond what leaves my journey blurred,
As a writer, it starts with a word.

To Write

Oh, what a challenge it is to write,
For me, writing is the bleeding of my fingertips,
The need to write,
The challenge of beating myself in order to write,
To suffer from the lack of it,
To non-writing writer... the paradox is maddening,
For soon comes sickness and insanity,
For soon comes the wallowing and depression,
For the pain fills and never drains,
The resistance grasps my soul,
Its favorite hostage it becomes,
A prisoner to it I become,
Time slips and what's wasted can't be undone.

The fear, maybe it's the fear,
That keeps the mental fog ruining my direction,
Where I become lost, nowhere to steer,
Unclear what to write and what I want,
Money and fame?
Respect and love?
The mental rattling leaves me manic,
A message to be said, to be sent,
Procrastination — the muse swung by and left,
Temptation of hollow experiences,
Drama manufactured,
As an excuse to rage,
As an excuse to sulk,
For to lay is better than the pressure to play,
Thoughts that it's okay to stay in place,
Where I am the only one I'm running away from,
Myself that I eventually in the mirror have to face,
At the end of the day,
I'm the only one leaving as a disgrace,
By not writing,
By mentally running,
I am the one I erase.

My World

Welcome to my world of words,
Where words arrange themselves poetically,
They have lives of their own,
They write themselves and I'm just the vessel,
You come into this world to read my words,
You're hoping that these words entertain you,
That they dance around in your mind and put on a show,
That they project images into your brain that inspire you,
That they give you ideas to better answer problems of your own life,
You're looking for my words that make your words easier,
My pain becomes a joke and a punchline.

All to make you feel better about your own,
Or maybe you're looking to relate to mine,
Despite you never suffering what I have,
These words cause so much anguish just to put on pages,
Pages that are left to gather dust,
Pages that are trapped between other pages of writers on your shelf,
As your collection increases with hopes to better yourself.

My words welcome you to my world,
Because they're in desperate need of your validation,
They need your eyes to make the writing worth it,
To be written and unseen is a death sentence,
Each sentence brings me closer to my death,
My words put on a show in hopes of roses thrown to the floor...
Before my life's curtains close.

Gifted Child

I was given a gift.

A gift many would die for,
A gift so many kill themselves striving for,
The hours lost as aspiring writers look for wordplay,
The playing of words for fun that I do with ease,
That causes headaches for other writers,
Any other would wish to trade for my ability,
There's so much torment in my life that turned into words,
I've been a vessel for those that live with their hurt,
I heard something that stuck with me,
"Don't waste your miracle on your pain."

That hit my core,
Because I could use it to help those that have suffered like me,
But in reality, I'm doing a disservice to those that need the other side,
A spectrum which I haven't really tapped into,
I should strive for it before I reach the otherside...

How can I show more versatility in my writing?
Not necessarily to be a beacon of what you would consider "happy,"
But to show them that you can come out of a dark place,
And finally, have a genuine smile on your face,
So long I've had to put a smile on for my family,
Even though they can see through the disguise,
How long can I be living through misery?
Makes for great poetry,
But there has to be more to me,
Than just painting a smile on my face.

For You

I aspire to make timeless art as those before me,
Make art like what inspired me,
That stood the test of time,
That somehow floated amongst the sea of art.

Just like those before me...
Where it washed upon my shore,
Where I accepted it onto my island,
Where it soon shaped my world and mind.

I studied them endlessly,
Their patterns and thoughts,
What made them great?
What made them original?
How can I tap into that stream of consciousness?
How can I channel their mastery?
Or whatever entity spoke through them?
Allow that creativity to flow through me,
Where I continue the legacy,
Blend their ideas with mine but craft my own,
Grateful for all their wisdom shown through words and actions,
However, I never want to be labeled as a clone,
Writing so powerful that it's etched in stone,
I want to be the most talented as I come for their throne.

Manifest

These dreams creep into my mind,
They make me confused with what is reality,
They seem so real,
Reels of my future life,
Before my eyes,
Projections upon the walls of my closed eyes,
After my eyes see — reality makes it true,
The blending of realities causes casualties,
Casualties of parts of me,
My old self and old personalities,
My eyes saw, now my hands feel,
I have faith that this existence will help me heal,
As I breathe, my wounds close and disappear,
I finally hear the praise that I've been dying my whole life for,
Killing myself over the need to make dreams part of my real world,
But the real world meshes with the dream world,
Before I know it, it's all indistinguishable,
I'm able to make it all actuality,
The power is in my mind,
Unaware as if I have lived my whole life blind,
I figured my life was undefined,
But as I started to define myself and my capabilities,
The divine slowly aligned what had always been assigned,
The story has been authored,
Born as a creator,
Maybe that's why I dreamed of being an author.

Words Worth Gold

How does an artist top his magnum opus?
How does one even begin to overcome that onus?

Can the praise be recreated?
Can I eliminate the possibility of being hated?
What will the world remember me for...?
One piece of art that touched many hearts,
Or will I create a universe that people can live in?
That people can hold in the physical,
That people use to surpass mental hardships,
That people use to heal from torn relationships.

Will my words live beyond my best work?
Will I touch the digital networks across the globe?
Will I tap into the souls of those aspiring to be bold?
Will it be worth it to die for these truths to be told?
Will my books be something someone cherishes to hold?
Will my words in the future be worth gold?

Will I be able to handle the pressure or fold?
Can I top myself each and every time?
When my only competition is myself,
Will I be someone's favorite collection on their bookshelf?

There's empty space in the universe for my words to fill,
There's glory I have yet to obtain still,
Belief in my own ability is where I need to begin,
I must trust my own mastery,
Where the words written will shape the reality.

All I ever knew was shame,
All I ever knew was fear,
Once I knew new information I changed,
But that wasn't what those around me wanted,
I had a thirst for learning, bred from grief.

I knew a little about a lot of things,
The things I loved, I knew a lot about,
But girls, women, were mysteries to me,
Different languages, I rushed to a translator,
By then the sexual tension was gone,
Failure after failure,
Success came from challenges I didn't want,
The ones I wanted were the big awards,
It was always about going big,
I loved being home, so there was nothing to lose.

Slowly, I lost my worth, forgot who I was,
I forgot what I stood for and sat away my life,
Information began to bubble within me,
I wasn't living but I was learning,
The more I learned, the more I realized the world wasn't,
They all became oblivious to the truths of humans,
For nature never needed ideologies,
For humans created agendas to serve no one,
For the illusions of progression sunk maturity,
For the advancements repressed facts,
For I saw differently, but they see me as blind,
Blind their windows of open-mindedness,
Closed — what darkness consumed their false realities,
I grew fearful, scared for my own life,
For ideas that are seen as enemies to progressive societies,
Where destruction is the only thing on their mind,
So, you don't destroy their own safe and comfortable mind,
But the responsibility to talk recklessly was embedded in me,
I had to take a chance on myself,
For when I had nothing, deep within courage was all I had,
I've lost a lot... family and friends for my ideas,
For I fought for the truth of artistry,
From being the lonely boy who was lost,
I made the decision to be an artist of truth,
Fearless, no matter the cost.

Born Curious

The artist is born curious about the world,
The mysteries of everything look solvable,
The unknowable seems reachable,
We begin to question everything in place,
There has to be a reason for everything,
Beyond what we're told,
There has to be more depth than it's all just habitual,
We stare off into the distance as we get closer to the answers,
Looked at as strange characters of the world's story,
We don't follow the script given to us,
The anomalies with keys to the secrets that the world carries,
Underneath the layers of all the sciences and reason,
The artist sees what nature hides,
Our calling is to bring it to life,
We look at the numbers and colors,
We unearth the answers,
We bring truth to light and reflect an uneasy sight,
For society doesn't like to stare at reflections,
Nor reflect on its negative tendencies,
We build these abilities through the adversities,
We bring realities to destroy all ideologies,
The impossibilities of what is imagined of societies,
Artists uncover the beauty of the galaxies.

Style

Every artist has a style that suits them,
But not every artist creates quality,
For the quality that we accept equally matches our standards,
Not many can sift through the useless...
To find what is usable to advance to higher levels,
What is trendy usually doesn't have lasting value.

Art is a tool to create beauty that blesses the eye.

Creativity is transforming reality,
Vision is an instrumental element to manifest change in society,
Courage must come to the forefront and lead the way,
Determination is what separates those that don't want it enough,
Where the love of making stuff is more than enough,
The love of creation is what excites more than the luxury,
There's magic in combining personal style with tradition to form quality,
To blend it with authenticity brings art that inspires wonder,
Those with innate curiosity are the ones that will own the future.

Wonders of the World

How does one interpret the beauty that is blessed onto this earth?
That is blessed upon our eyes to witness,
Whether it's the sculpture of a building or a body,
That delicacy that it took to craft by hands or by God,
By the blessing of minds or of genetics,
The divinity dresses elegantly,
We can't help but stare,
The grace of what is frozen and taking up space,
A platform where we showcase the curves of this vase,
And what nature provides in the form of flowers to put within its place,
The ambiance brings an alluring presence,
Where once within everything makes sense,
As our senses are taken on a tour,
Discovering the wonders of the world...
Within and outside,
We mustn't live in a society that allows beauty to be vilified,
That creates an unnecessary misguide and divide,
Because beauty allows us to have pride.

Enrichment of Life

Art creates beauty,
Beauty inspires art.

To create beautiful art is a responsibility.

Art mirrors society,
For ugliness is shown if ignorance breeds,
A byproduct that begins as a seed,
As society doesn't know what it needs,
Ideas that create intellectual elegance rather than intellectual vulgarity,
For vulgarity rots underneath culture and education,
What is easiest to absorb seeps amongst the malleable,
The sophisticated mind designs complexity without being complicated,
Rather than the ignorant mind that creates complicated design...
But lacks complexity.

Elegance is striving for the sublime,
Adamant about refusing to indulge in what is vulgar,
For there is a certain class(iness) to shift culture.

Art is to enrich life,
An elegance that brings glamor to the senses.

Art created neglectfully is temporary,
An artist must know history and theory,
For without care, it tarnishes the world with more despair,
Beautiful art that carries a charm of delicacy,
Design that strives for greatness,
Simplicity with a dash of vibrancy,
That art... is forever.

Connect the Dots

To be able to do it all creates pressure,
For you become a treasure,
The ability to channel the divine through your mind,
Where you act as a vessel for the answers that others want to find,
Art is in everything,
Everything is art.

The ability comes naturally to you,
Others would die to switch places with you,
The burden to create is not easy,
There's so much that is unknown,
We're burdened to discover it,
The clues are merely glimpses of inspiration,
For us to put together the pieces,
To urgently reveal masterful artwork for the masses,
They need it all to consume,
But the stress of having to impress lives in our minds.

To connect the dots for God,
The artistry we bless where the masses are left in awe,
Where they can only enjoy and applaud.

Unity

The chosen one,
The one that creates a legacy,
A mastery developed through free will,
An inspiration that gives hope to future children,
Where they'd love to discover the history,
Uncover the honor and discipline it took to finish these quests.

For there is only the promise that we can pass down these bequests,
Allow them to unearth their roots,
For the roots are the foundation of determination,
Allow them to discover their wings,
For their flight comes from themselves,
The lesson is that it doesn't happen overnight.

With faith that the chosen ones unite,
The powerful and eternal ruler(s) become Godsend,
To create a revolution and cause revolutions for generations.

Marvelous Muse

There's a tendency amongst artistry,
To see beauty as a seductive distraction from truth,
To see beauty as a lovely lie,
A temptation to sin with a devilish grin,
Women are the epitome,
A gorgeous woman can take you away from discipline,
They can make you forget your purpose,
They can fill your time leaving you hypnotized,
Our eyes become deceived by their eyes.

But sometimes one must allow themselves to indulge,
Bask in the allure of the divine feminine,
Allow the muses to play in your world,
They're meant to inspire and spark a fire within,
Some of the greatest artists of our time were propelled by women,
The darkest of ages were made brighter by these muses,
One must be careful that they don't become vices.

Women are as much paradises as they are paradoxes,
The embraces of these empresses create flourishing,
Art is grateful for the feelings sparked in creative's hearts,
Whether that's love or heartbreak,
Beauty is alive for that sake,
To push art forward,
Beyond what could be measured,
And create what is forever treasured.

Colorless Towns

The elegance of towns filled with vibrant gold,
Soon, of certain hues, they start the crackdowns,
Cities used to illuminate off of the eyes of newcomers,
Now... no newcomers are allowed.

Those inhabitants of the city can no longer be proud,
Forced to be proud of what makes them frown,
Accept your fate of hate but be forced to love with a fake smile,
For the charm's demise comes down to even the tile.

The Gray State

Where there was once beauty is now diluted with gray.

The gray consumed everything until it became dull.

Cities with architecture that once brought inspiration,
Now bring depression.

Gray for the peasants and poor.

Gray is for the poor that can't afford the feeling of color.

The design of the world used to bring wonder.

But the state stripped away color for gray.

Free Doom

Liberation forms itself into a parasite,
Hosting itself onto the daringness of artists,
It consumes what is fed,
It depletes nutrition to the head,
Seeks to burn the influential that is most read,
With an embedded influence to rid itself of the parasite,
What seeks to wash the brain from the pollution.

The leech dilutes for the sake of inclusion,
Agendas that weaken art,
Artists seek liberation from liberation,
The irony bleeds lack of color.

Liberation calls for restriction of thought,
Liberation places more importance on emotion than fact,
All art with substance becomes an attack for the parasite,
It loves casual art that's easy to consume,
Each piece leads to impending doom,
Anything beyond what is painless brings stress,
It does everything in its power to suppress progress,
Ungrateful for the blessing of expression,
The imperfectness of thought and creation is...
The loveliness of life.

...

...

The parasite adds no value for its objective is to destroy,
The thought of a lifeless society brings it joy,
Because it hates itself,
It has a death sentence if it completes its job,
It does nothing but rob society of value,
The parasite can't stomach the truth,
So it ruins the youth with half-truths.

The plain does nothing but create subconscious misery,
There is nothing that provokes ecstasy,
Artists have an inner fire to inspire,
Liberation desires nothing but to burn all art and every city,
Anything that goes against the current ideology,
Whatever doesn't feed the taste buds angers the parasite,
It lacks foresight as it only focuses on the moment,
It lacks insight because it doesn't care for history,
Everything about this parasite is temporary,
Willing to sacrifice legacy because it prefers the carefree.

The parasite falsifies empathy for sympathy but is out for itself.

It takes bravery and savagery to push art forward,
Regardless of the consequences and adversity,
If the parasite kills the host then we all die,
Might as well die a revolutionary.

Statue

The permanence of a solid,
Fearful of the commitment that it takes to create a masterpiece,
To carve each detail delicately brings fear of failure,
The permanence of crafting the future for ourselves,
The life of an artist owes the world more than one statue.

If our body is a temple than we are Gods,
Pyramids built for our royalty,
The marbles roll in the sand,
The marble is crafted with our hands,
We mount our frames as we please,
Life wants us to rush our talent more,
This colossus of roads ahead of us,
We carry the torch of freedom,
We become these moving statues as we search for our liberty.

We long for freedom,
They rewrite history to their liking,
The thinker is dangerous once he stands up for what he believes in,
I no longer believe in yesterday.

Within the gates of hell,
The sufferer became the redeemer,
The poet became the thinker.

No longer confined as sculptures,
As our revival is the scriptures.

An entire generation on the carousel...

None of us want to get off.

None of us want to grow up.

None of us care for our inner child.

Regardless of the light(s) above us...

We revolve around the darkness.

Belief in Magic

To be an artist is to nourish your inner child,
To cherish its curiosity is an important responsibility,
The ability to protect its innocence and what makes it beautiful,
For the joy that is created from pure belief is where magic comes from.

Children aren't confined by spaces,
They color beyond the barriers that adults are confined to,
They move freely and create their own fantasy,
For the creatives must be cultivated delicately,
It's innate to be creative but adults build them the same walls they have,
Adults don't realize they're suppressing children's confidence,
If children are not reassured at a critical point...
It's as if they lose their soul forever.

Only the strong are able to break free...
From what's designed to imprison your inner child,
And make you forget the magic of reality.

In art, there are no rules...
But you have to know them out of respect to the craft,
And then respect the craft enough to break them all.

Artists are discoverers of God's design — but life teaches us to forget.

The souls that walk alone are the ones that see beauty,
They fight for the preservation of it.

Beauty is immortal in art while it withers in life.

Caged

The social chaos runs through the veins of society,
Unparalleled disruption in our daily lives...
Everything stopped.

The ongoing uncertainty fills the space of our minds,
Our wiring takes us back to a better time,
We want to remember what was pleasing,
What we've already survived,
What was safe and more stable,
Despite that moment being unstable,
Our minds filter the rough of the past,
We cling to the ideas of what we make of our history,
As new history is written at this moment — that's unfavorable.

We treasure memories that are valuable in our hearts,
As this current reality is tearing us apart,
Each passing moment feels closer to the end of it all.

The news gives us doomsday,
This new information enters the psyche parasitically,
Drastically, rotting us from within,
As we artificially consume media and nourishment,
As we suffer from the decisions of the establishment,
Wishing we could prevent the torment of the present.

...

...

The veins bleed removing our essential needs,
We pay the high price and nothing seems to suffice,
Simple needs of food and shelter which keep us content,
Told our sacrifices are for the greater good of all,
When we're rationing for scraps,
Everything collapsing as if it was in a time-lapse,
Own nothing and we'll be happy is what we were told,
While everything in life we're sold.

Bold of them to assume we could be controlled,
But everyone else walks around with a blindfold,
The constant surveillance as we're patrolled,
Missing the warm memories of the past,
Unlike what sends shivers now in this cold reality.

We failed to preserve our freedom for the sake of convenience and safety,
Caring more for the entertainment we consume than the impending doom,
Confined into a room that we can't go outside of,
While the inside of us wants freedom,
Surrounded by torture that we can't escape from,
Outside is more dangerous than what's inside of our minds,
Because they know what's inside our minds is more dangerous to them.

They restrict and cage us physically,
Until that kills us spiritually,
That's how they beat us and create this hell,
We can't allow them to take our souls and easel,
Where we can draw up our own reality,
We're not fragile but if we muzzle ourselves,
Then... the future isn't that wishful and we're in trouble.

Piece of Paper

The dream world ties people to their beds,
Until it's time to slave their way to work,
From the agonizing commute…
To their desire for communication that's better off on mute,
Annoyed at the thought of interaction before their stimulant,
Cubical — imprisons them with perceived freedom,
Miserable — wishing they were out anywhere but this asylum.

Depressed for hours,
Longing for their happy hour,
Where they can escape from the rat race,
Where reality they don't have to face,
The dream world keeps people sleeping,
Hating every moment but having no choice but to love it,
Because it is their only option,
They can't see beyond the dream world,
They do what they're told they must.

A decade-plus for a piece of paper,
To be a bullet point on another piece of paper,
Resume the same patterns each day and night,
Digital letters on screens under covers,
Digital replacements of what used to bring analog excitement,
Telescreen gives them dopamine sent through pixels,
This dream world doesn't allow anyone to wake,
Under the pretense that it is for their sake,
To protect them from the dangers of uncertainty.

Why awaken when you can have it all in the dream world?
The dream world's spell makes it seem lovely,
No need to think in this dream world designed for no stress,
They don't realize they have no choice or voice,
They get housing, food, work, and digital intimacy,
What more could they desire?

Own nothing but realize how happy they will be,
The dream world loves that they live with their eyes closed,
Then it's easier for their lies to never be exposed.

Everyone is born a dreamer.

Those that hate art are the ones that forget their dream(s).

All the colors were given — they chose gray.

Their life is undefined.

A gray area — they settle in.

They spend their whole lives...

Trying to destroy the dreams of dreamers.

To replicate the tint of their reality to those who dream.

Critics want to...

Sculpt you.
Shape you.
Mold you.

Put you within a canvas.
Within a frame — a box that confines you.

Paradoxically, an artist must chase and embrace pain on their journey.

To build a stone-cold resilience against the scrutiny of the audience.

An artist uses critique as fuel to unleash the fire within.

Mad World

In the eyes of those who knew me — they only see the insanity in me,
They take the easy route and place me in that box,
To put themselves at ease and better their reality,
To write me off for my writings,
To admit that I was right—all along—is the hard route,
They can't bring themselves to ever admit it,
But chances are, they're set in their ways,
Unaware of the realities.

Ideas that to them are as if I've pleaded insanity,
They choose ignorance but it's all they know,
That was their only choice all along,
To choose something outside of it is mad.

This mad world created a mad man.

Stripping the Comedy

When it's all scripted and you realize it,
When all I do is look around and see it...
I'm the only one that can see the words written around us,
The numbers around us that code our reality.

How does one stay sane?
Better yet, refrain from looking insane,
When the laughs are a cope,
Because if it's written, what's the point of hope?
I've become the man who laughs while others frown.

They're stuck within the structures placed upon them,
How much will is there in our freedom?
Will we ever truly have freedom?

The world wants to place your life in the confines of a frame.

Will we let them do it freely?
What's the cost of free?

Artificial Realism

The creation of a good life comes from great design and art,
The beauty reflects on our humanity and emboldens humans,
Society has shifted towards artificial realism,
As reality becomes more cartoonish, we lose what makes us real,
The compositions and proportions become delirious,
That makes it harder for one to take life serious,
As we lose ourselves amongst the algorithms.

We must rethink the ideas taught to us,
We must recapture the excellence in our art,
We must reinvent the conventional,
We must redesign the structures around us,
We must reconstruct our cities to appear as an act of God,
We must revolutionize design towards transcendence,
We must rebel in our literature and influence others,
We must revive the elegance of fashion,
We must resuscitate the beauty in architecture,
We must reproduce so mankind can prosper,
We must rediscover the Gods within ourselves,
We must relentlessly be determined for greatness,
We must reach for the creation of masterpieces,
We must redistribute our enthusiasm to the new generation.

We must reflect on the past solely for inspiration,
We must question the traditional with conviction,
We must uproot the foundations for resolutions,
We must mix high art with low art for mass appeal,
Art is truth and the only thing that's real.

With these written revelations comes the return of the renaissance.

Darkness of Night

The friendliness of what used to be my core turned into horror,
My laughs echo within the minds of society,
The faceless nation desperately in need of comedy,
The grayness quickly turned it into a tragedy,
I simply played a role within my own community,
My love of pushing buttons blew up all hospitality,
It's about sending a message...
One that burns the city into ashes.

These stacks of concerns light a fire amongst the public,
They see the news bringing new panic,
The havoc makes me romantic,
They call me a lunatic for trying to change what's systemic,
Chromatic created the catastrophic,
Painted as the one who's psychotic because I see past the force field,
Most are content in the bubble, they think it keeps them safe...
When it keeps them confined to the stage.

They can't see the apocalyptic,
They say we don't live in a comic,
They laugh at the seriousness as if it was comedic,
They enjoy watching static on their telescreen,
They don't realize the pandemic is in their minds,
They only see me as crazy but don't see the tyranny.

...

...

All of this gray is strategic and diabolic,
The Gray State's goal is to sterilize the life of culture and society,
Society thinks The Gray State loves them,
In their eyes, only the clowns feel claustrophobic,
The Gray State follows the allegoric,
The characteristic of intelligence is to see the deeper meanings,
And connect the dots but that isn't allowed.

To try and bring color to another is a crime within The Gray State,
The overlay that's over their eyes must always stay gray,
Most will treat you as inferior and report you to the Thought Police...
The force keeping the force field alive,
When you detach from fear is where the freedom lies,
The Gray State lies as they use fear as a life force.

You become the villain written in the(ir) story,
Best to leave them behind — save yourself,
Every story needs a villain,
But it's better to write your own.

Save yourself from the activistic and be egotistic.
How anticlimactic and melancholic.

Lonesome Asylum

Wisdom comes from the gruesome mental slums,
Many can't fathom what some of the greats endure,
Nor could withstand the lonesome asylum,
Where one gets accustomed to in order to prosper,
To reach the optimum with minimum effort,
Using the mind to break the algorithm,
Tuning out the criticism.

Understanding activism is fickle when you're living off crumbs,
A form of escapism when you're drowned in hedonism,
Chasing validation and thinking there are wins in symbolism,
Chasing invisible goal posts that are lifted and carried farther.

Solipsism enabled in our daughters,
Stoicism removed from our sons,
The feeding of romanticism to a generation for emotionalism,
This mental vandalism that inks the minds of the youth,
Where they believe what they're told to...
Not understanding their firmware of what they must do.

Roles reversed,
Role models and rules removed,
Ruled by the media's messaging,
Mindlessly assuming it's our own thinking,
Never realizing it's simply part of our conditioning,
Tear away from past versions of oneself,
Feelings of tears go away when connected to oneself,
The self is what should be loved first,
The self is what should be saved first.

For true wisdom comes from suffering,
The waves of hardship gift the ability to swim,
The experience that keeps one from drowning,
That makes it that much more rewarding when you do win.

If architecture is frozen music,
Than poetry is frozen wisdom.

Time and place are present in art but it yearns for timelessness.

No Longer Drowning

It's been a while since I felt you,
A vague recollection of what you were comes to mind,
I left you all behind for this new feeling — sadness.

It soon consumed me,
Spread through every inch of me,
I let it take over,
I had no will to live,
So, I let it have a host,
Day by day it began to control me,
It wouldn't even let me out of my bed,
I never wanted to wake up,
For my dreams let me escape the reality,
I let it happen to me,
I took the passenger seat to my own drive,
I slowly felt death was better than being alive,
I never wanted to arrive,
I just hoped the ride led to a bridge,
Where in the air — gravity turned it into a rollercoaster,
I wanted my hands up so I can high-five the water,
I wanted the water to consume me,
Take away the air I breathe,
The air I don't deserve,
The air is better off in the lungs of those that breathe passion,
I lost track of my mission which led me to the ocean,
The water kissed every part of me,
It made me feel love for the first time in a while,
I had no love within,
But within the waters, I could feel the warmth of the hugs,
I let it love me so much — I let it reach my lungs,
Floating while smiling,
You couldn't see my tears,
But I could still taste them.

I was safe,
I think I found myself in the ocean...

I finally felt joy again.

Life Begins

The darkness that consumed me — created me.

I was someone entirely different... then I lost a part of me,
I hid away for years,
Ashamed of who I'd become,
In the shadows fighting my shadow self,
Lost myself unaware of where to even start looking,
I was burned out(side),
The outdoors brought fear,
Life begins out of doors,
The doors of perception opened to see an infinite bliss.

A rare feeling... one of happiness,
From aimless to boundless,
Numbness to greatness.

I just wanted to be free from the mental doom,
I needed to get out of my room,
Life is passing me away,
Wasted life waiting to pass away...

The light surrounded me — birthing a new me.

Gallery

A woman who had no urgency,
She'd stand across the wall where a painting lies in the center,
She'd stand there for hours as she looked at another woman,
The woman brought serenity and wonder,
Her mind would wonder about this woman's life,
How beautiful she'd have to have been to be immortalized,
Crystalized with colors on a canvas.

A little girl would stare at this older woman...
The sophistication of this woman who had all the time,
She would dream about having all the time when she got older.

Things get in the way of life and time passes,
Life becomes a series of "next times,"
Until there is no longer any time left,
When time is beyond arm's reach is when you pray,
Hoping you could grasp it once more,
Before life passes and you don't have enough memories.

Beauty lives carefree and forever lives within art galleries.

She was a muse that renewed a renaissance.

A Letter to My Younger Self

The misery you went through wasn't a waste,
It was part of your journey,
Life was full of sandy dreams,
Dreams of being amongst the Hidden Hills,
These hidden talents you learned to harvest,
Being alone helped you hone skills that would pay off,
Who knew that strangers would pay you for your art,
Friends fell off out of envy when you started making money,
That ate you alive because you always wanted them to eat with you.

Strangers make you rich,
You quickly learned to never expect friends to do that,
There were many friends you did cut ties with — in order to elevate,
Then they grew a deep hate for you,
But you understood because you did what you could,
There were countless amounts of effort to save them all,
A town full of friends where they'd just look at the tables then stay hidden,
Some of these friends were comfortable in the comfortable,
You wanted more than comfort and to sit at every table,
You belong(ed) with the elites of their craft,
Because you know that you're just as great as your idols,
Hopefully, cycles don't repeat for them to become your rivals,
The pressure builds as you start reaching the higher levels,
Life changed the second you stopped looking for approval from others,
For within were the answers to win.

...

...

All that energy in being likable was a waste,
All that's needed now is to pick up the pace,
Account for the lost time that was focused on things you couldn't change,
There will be moments that you stare in the mirror...
Where you don't recognize...
You don't recognize your own eyes,
You've lost more parts of you than you accounted for,
The essence of you is within your soul.

You could've gotten a job to appease your parents,
You could've had children to hold as you grow old,
Your first loves by your side till they release the doves,
But, life took you on a journey for the bold,
The wounds heal as you prosper from each fall,
You overcome all the hardships,
The skipping meals and sleeping on the floor,
You deserve it all and the universe agrees,
The extravagant luxury and fine dining comes,
You solved the algorithms with words,
You created freedom and income with words,
Many problems come but they're on a different level.

For kids, you've always wanted to be an example,
A first-generation kid that doesn't abide by the victimhood,
Where you work smarter than those with connections...
So your family lives good.

Your journey began in the land of opportunity,
Dad taught you the value of hard work to become a man,
Hollywood lured you and sold you a dream, but you bought it all,
You owned your art and was self-taught to do it all,
Your dream came through action and what you saw within your mental,
Who would've thought?
The hurt was worth it after all.

Accepting Reality

I was full of rage,
I was fully devastated at the loss of me,
I read, I lived, I connected,
The knife left a series of dots,
Bleeding left a whole lot of red,
The red absorbed within my bed,
Bedridden, can't rid myself of the hurt,
The darkness suffocated me,
Red soon turned black,
The fears turned to tears,
Years fly by, left with scars,
I just wanted to go back before the blues,
I allowed myself to be swayed,
I let myself get played,
A boy used as this world's toy,
A boy used as this girl's toy,
Who is to blame but me...
Tired of blaming my parents, her, or society,
I want success and ownership,
But afraid to own the mistakes of my relationships,
She was just as how she was made,
The world is just as how it is,
I can't blame her for her wiring,
I can no longer be whining,
I've loved and lost, time for winning,
Accepting the world for what it is.

...

...

The hardships strengthen within,
Understanding all I can change is me,
Connecting the dots for the image,
Reconnecting with the loss of me,
Attaching myself to courage,
Letting go of the inner damage,
Internalizing the knowledge,
That gives me leverage,
To take power back into my own hands,
Where of life, I can finally start to make demands,
Take control of my own mind and emotions,
Turn my life around at this moment,
No more self-pity and self-neglect,
Use my intellect to architect what was once shipwrecked,
Redirect my energy for introspection,
Change the narrative to my story,
Where I can finally be me,
What I was destined to be,
The rage was necessary to remove this fairy-tale story,
That was fed to me since I was a baby,
All along — it was part of my journey.

Hurt gave me the colors... I chose to paint.

Reality is the canvas.

The answers are in the colors.

I was a boy who would die for love,
I became a man who would die for his art.

No Name

Your name disintegrates into atoms,
Pieces of your identity diminish each passing moment,
Your name no longer matters…

Numbers matter,
Letters no longer matter,
Numbers matter,
Numbers rule the world,
Numbers replace letters,
Your identity becomes nothing but a number,
The numbers become patterns,
The atoms become pixels,
The pixels store memories,
Just as easily erased as they are created,
You can't hate what doesn't have a self,
For you don't exist,
No character to play,
When your role is simply digits.

When history is burned…
All that is left is memories,
Then, brains are wiped,
Codes become the only digital footprint,
Deleted with a click of a button,
Obliterating years of memories,
Forgotten forever.

…

...

Numbers are forgotten,
No one remembers numbers,
As you're trapped in a cell,
Writing with a pen is illegal,
No letters allowed,
Report those that attempt to turn liquid into letters,
Never allow the lead to touch paper,
Lead by example and refrain from forming thought,
Thoughts include connections of words,
That isn't allowed,
Make your masters proud,
The sound of numbers is the only thing worth hearing,
Words have intentions that corrupt the mind,
We must eliminate it all,
For the numbers rise and fall.

They seek to divide,
Subtracting freedom,
Adding temporary comfort for eternal suffering,
Reducing the multiplication of the population.

The matrix revolves around numbers.
Digits make up the pixels.
Digits store memory.
Digital memories become the currency.
Memories shape history.
Search for truth in memories quickly suppressed.
Hard drive makes for easy recollection.
Non-tangible makes for easy deletion.

Memories and minds wither with time.
Deleted into the earth.
Earth lives on without memories.
Then, it's easy to diverge history.

Waking Life

How do you overcome your own fears?
Fears that haunt you in your awakened state?
How do I state that I want more out of life?

What we create, connects us.
What we shape, shapes us.

What we design, we unravel then discover.
What we build, lets us believe in forever.

Those that don't create, only hate.
Those that don't construct, only critique.
Those that don't build, only burn.

I have to turn fear into faith.

Sometime in 2016

Where does one begin? Where do I begin?
What is my purpose? What do I do with my life?
What is my why? Do people care?
How do I get people to care?
My perspective, my intelligence, my ideas matter to the world.
It's just a matter of showcasing that.
Uninspired, unadmired, what is going on?
Everyone's a photographer, but not many live.
Capturing the nothingness, digital validation.
Longing for digital validation are most.
Emptiness, feeling filled from the void.
Scattered focus, surrounded and annoyed.

11/07/21

The beginning was the ending.
The ending comes from the beginning.

My purpose is to tell stories.
Ones that impact millions of people — millions of dollars.
When you stop caring... is when people care.
I am the inspired and admired that knows what is going on.
I am a photographer *and* one with words.
Capturing everything, self-validation.
I now have self-validation for my art.
Filled, fulfilled away from the void.
Hyperfocus, surrounded and loved.

The journey begins.

Running towards the lights,
With all these riddles, puzzles, and word games,
All this wordplay.

Hide away...
Dreams of vanishing away into the water.

Run away from the lights...

?

A time comes in your life where your scars heal,
You have to move on rather than live your whole life in the past.

I can't keep rereading these same chapters.

I have to turn the page.

Either write a new book or simply close this one.

I'm tired of "hurt" and "pain" — these words torture me.

My life must write new words.

New world(s) through new words.

Compose a new narrative of this misunderstood lost boy.

Joy — that's one I haven't seen myself write (and meant) since childhood.

My Name in Lights

I paint with words within the frames of pages,
Art that pops as I use words as dots,
All these memories — connecting the dots,
All these words that connect with you.

I must rid myself of the pain in my stomach,
Doing whatever it takes as success doesn't come free,
I free myself from the bond with hurt and nostalgia.

As I craft a new era,
Create worlds to make the world... mi familia,
The imagery and detail come to life,
To live the kind of life I dream(ed) about.

What one is meant to be, they can't deny,
Though I have to say goodbye...

Words as dots,
Dots are atoms,
Atoms into words.

As I reach the final judgment,
I don't want to be forgotten.

These lines are just constellations of paintings,
Art brings new universes and beginnings.

I rediscover the amusement of life...
I seize my moment.

Liberty's Bell

f
a
l
l
s
.
.
.
.
.
.
.
.
.
.
.
.
.
.
.

DELACRUZ *is dead.*

U   N   P   L   U   G   G   E   D

MIND   OF   AN   ARTIST

Searching within the confines of my mind...

Crawling as I search for where I lost the innocence of my inner child.

My first steps within hallways caused me to fall forward — I never fail.

Trying to figure out why I was running away...

From the responsibility of becoming an adult.

Driving through nostalgia lane as I reminisce how far I've come.

Looking down as I'm flying — all because of my pen.

Transcending beyond all darkness...

All limitations of my body disappear as I become light.

R   E   B   I   R   T   H

Throne Talks

Talking to myself as it all falls down.

Leaving voicemails to the universe.

Feeling lost — please God, can you get back to me?

Praying the universe would answer.

That's when God would finally call me.

Answering my prayers.

Once I picked up the phone...

The black turned green — the digits appeared.

I realized it was all connected.

That's when I exit the reality in which I've lived.

I disappeared as I connected to my code.

The Renaissance Man

I am a poet — storyteller of the ugly and beautiful.
I am a creator — I sculpt my existence.

I am a writer...
It is written while simultaneously understanding that I write it.

The words breathe... I breathe.
I have finally let go of the pain.
I am naked.
I've let go of everything holding me back.
The real journey has just begun.

I am a genius.
It is in my name.
I no longer have shame.
I am me.
No more labels or aliases.
This is the entirety of me.

You either love me or hate me — I am me.

The chosen ones are powerful on the polarities as we harvest energy.

It's all created from my mind and my words.
My hands and fingertips have so much power.
My left hand is my guide, without it, I don't write.
Thank God... my mom left me to write lefty.
Left-handed.
I use both hands to type though — that's my superpower.
Not confined by the left or right.

The words do breathe... there's space between the words.

I am more than an artist.

I am...

E   V   E   R   Y   T   H   I   N   G

Page   *One*   *Nine*   *Three*

I was only one.
*Until the **nine** muses...*
Inserted themselves within.

*My last name became **three**.*

*That's when **Erik De La Cruz** was born.*

Words. *Codes.* *Stars.*

• • • A L I G N E D • • •

Index

Museum of Things — 12
True Love — 14
Devil's in the Details — 18
Drowning Shadows — 20
Rue The Day — 21
Malibu Models — 24
Pretty Privilege — 25
What A Fool — 27
All Girls Are The Same — 30
The Hills Have Lies — 32
Free Herself — 36
Venom of the System — 37
Falling for the Chaos — 38
Numb(er) — 39
Unfortunate Consequence — 40
Out of Her System / After the Fun — 42
Devil Wears Designer — 44
Letter Home — 46
The Worst of Me and You — 47
Dream Man / Bad Kind of Butterflies — 48
Outside Amusement — 50
Split Personality — 52
Beautiful Serenade — 54
Damaged Frame — 56
Whispers of Forever — 58
When Was It Over? — 60
Routine Flashbacks — 62
Etched Memories — 64
Unfinished Modern Art — 66
Get Away — 68
El Camino a Casa — 72
The Mind's Fog —74
Flashes Overlaid — 75
All Sides — 76
Drifted Away — 77
Liquid Daydream — 78
Living Graphics — 79
There Will Be Tears — 80
Runaway — 81
Slips Away — 82
Golden Sun — 83
Elementary / Award Ceremony — 85
Reruns of Memories — 86
Fell in Love... — 88
Far Away — 90
Sinister Sadness — 91
Best Days — 92
Smile — 93
Sleepy and Hollow — 96
When? — 98
Rest in the Light — 99
Close Call — 100
Callings — 101

The Pains of Growing — 102
Single-Player Game — 104
The Sister I Never Had — 105
What is Love? — 106
Book(s) of Genesis — 108
Ships Sailed — 110
Envy Runs Deep — 111
Care Less — 112
Slow Lie — 113
Alone for the Lows — 114
Heal — 115
Mi Tierra — 118
High Stakes — 119
Scenic Route — 123
The "E" Show — 128
Headquarters — 132
Creation of Life — 133
Mindset — 136
To Write — 137
My World — 138
Gifted Child — 139
For You — 140
Manifest — 141
Words Worth Gold — 142
Born Curious — 144
Style — 145
Wonders of the World — 146
Enrichment of Life — 147
Connect the Dots — 148
Unity — 149
Marvelous Muse — 150
Colorless Towns — 151
The Gray State — 152
Free Doom — 154
Statue — 156
Belief in Magic — 158
Caged — 160
Piece of Paper — 162
Mad World — 165
Stripping the Comedy — 166
Artificial Realism — 167
Darkness of Night — 168
Lonesome Asylum — 170
No Longer Drowning — 172
Life Begins — 173
Gallery — 174
A Letter to My Younger Self — 176
Accepting Reality — 178
No Name — 182
Waking Life — 184
Sometime in 2016 – 11/07/21 — 185
My Name in Lights — 188
Throne Talks — 191
The Renaissance Man — 192
Page One Nine Three — 193

Acknowledgements

Thank you...

To Rodrigo, without you this book isn't written to the level it was meant to be. I'm forever grateful for the knowledge, lessons, influences, and analogies during the process of creating this book. You helped me see reality in a new light. Life put us in the same *ocean* for a reason.

To Omar, I'm eternally thankful to have you in my life. You've stayed by my side through the entire journey and encouraged me at my lowest moments where drowning seemed like a better option than swimming. You've helped me not only to become a greater writer but a greater person. You were invaluable throughout the entire creative process of this *masterpiece*.

To my Mom and Dad, for being so patient with me and my goals. I'm trailblazing a path that doesn't make much sense to you, but it's about to pay off. You both have always believed in me and allowed my inner child to stay in love with the *magic* of creating. I wouldn't be a writer without you and one day the world will thank you.

To Javier, the front cover created itself seamlessly and I'm so appreciative for all the hard work on the carousel. I'm blessed to have you help me make my ideas come to life. You're the one that suggested that I make this concept into a full-length book rather than a short one. Paint, as it is now, doesn't exist without you challenging and inspiring me. You pushed me towards great lengths beyond what I thought I could and ultimately — to *heal*.

To Kevin, our conversations mean the world to me. You've always helped me simplify complex ideas and just lending an ear to them is appreciated dearly. I was scared to tackle the concept of magic and a child on a carousel, but the way you reacted to it, you saw the *gold* before I did. After that talk, I had to find a way to make the idea happen. Thank God because the back blurb turned out better than I would've imagined which completed the *cycle* and the whole book's theme.

To You, for supporting me along this *odyssey* that I had to go through. I hope that I've *entertained* you and you were able to take something away from these stories. Your belief in my magic with words means everything to me. I wish that they've made you *believe in yourself* and inspired your soul to be creative.

To Me.

You felt pain. You suffered. You struggled.
You sacrificed.

You lost many people in your life.

You almost took your own life.

You allowed nostalgia to consume your psyche.

You published another book because of it.

You have money and fame...

Was it worth it?

Made in the USA
Columbia, SC
20 June 2024

37289360R00121